FREDERIC OZANAM

AND THE ESTABLISHMENT

OF THE

SOCIETY OF ST. VINCENT DE PAUL

BY

ARCHIBALD J. DUNN

F.R.Hist.S., F.G.S., etc.

British Library Cataloguing-in-Publication Data
A catalogue record for this book is available from
the British Library

TO

HIS EMINENCE

FRANCIS, CARDINAL BOURNE

ARCHBISHOP OF WESTMINSTER AND PATRON OF THE SOCIETY OF
ST. VINCENT DE PAUL IN ENGLAND

THIS BOOK IS MOST RESPECTFULLY DEDICATED BY

THE AUTHOR

PREFACE

THE life of Antoine Frederic Ozanam, as given in the following pages, was written by me in 1877, and published in that year. I derived the information contained in it from my friend, George Jonas Wigley, who was a favourite pupil of Ozanam's and his constant correspondent until his death.

Thus, although I had not the advantage of having known Ozanam personally, I always kept in touch with him and his ideas through Wigley, and upon these I have based my theory as to the scope of the Society of St. Vincent de Paul as an international agency to direct the future of emigrants to Catholic centres.

I am indebted to the *Catholic Times* for permission to publish their report of the Centenary Meeting at Manchester, and to the editor of the *Bulletin* for the report of that in Paris.

CONTENTS

ix

CHAPTER I

LIFE OF FREDERIC OZANAM

CHAPTER I

LIFE OF FREDERIC OZANAM

CATHOLIC historians of future times, when they come to pass in review the names of the men who have most distinguished themselves in the battle of the Church against Paganism in France, will single out those of Montalembert, Lacordaire, Veuillot, De Broglie, and De Falloux, as having taken the most prominent places in the public eye. But they will find no life more worthy of study or of admiration, as an example of the good which can be done by a simple layman in his sphere, than that of Frederic Ozanam, the founder of the Society of St. Vincent de Paul. The full measure of the good which has been done to the Catholic cause, not only in France, but throughout the world, by the unpretentious working of that great Society, is known only to God. But in France especially it has proved the most powerful barrier to the spread of irreligion, scepticism, and the class prejudices and suspicions which were engendered by the Revolution. For the principles of the Society are the promotion of the love of God and our fellow-men, and its fruits

are an unostentatious philanthropy and a spirit of
conciliation, which are in themselves the noblest
vindication of Christianity.

Frederic Ozanam was born at Milan on April 13,
1813. His father was a Frenchman of ancient
lineage, who had left Paris upon the proclamation
of the first Empire, in disgust at the treachery of
Napoleon; he had served during the Italian cam-
paign in a hussar regiment, and had shared in the
glories of Lodi, Arcola, Pavia, Rivoli, etc. Owing
to a sudden reverse of fortune, he had been compelled to seek employment as a professor at Milan,
where he afterwards took his degrees as a doctor of
medicine. When Milan was ceded to the Austrians,
Dr. Ozanam returned with his family to Lyons, the
home of his wife's relations, and soon established a
good practice there. He was a man of true piety,
and devoted his life to works of charity among the
poor, whom he attended gratuitously and helped out
of his own small fortune, and in this he was ably
seconded by his wife.

His son, Frederic, was distinguished from his
earliest childhood by great sensitiveness and kindness of heart, and by the earnest piety which had
been instilled into him by the example and precepts
of his saintly mother, which formed the solid foundation for the achievements of his after-life and his
consolation in all his trials. At school he showed
an earnestness and intelligence which gave promise

of a brilliant future. At seventeen years of age he
had gone through his curriculum of study with
great distinction. During his years of rhetoric and
philosophy he experienced the bitter trials of unrest,
and the temptations to scepticism which so often
afflict earnest and thinking minds in youth. These
temptations made a deep and lasting impression on
his mind, and he spoke in after-years of " the horror
of those doubts that eat into the heart, pursuing us
even at night to the pillow we have drenched with
our tears." After suffering for a long time, he felt
impelled to seek the only source of solace and relief
which can be found.

Miss Kathleen O'Meara, in the biography which she
published, tells us the story in the following words :
" One day, when the temptation was at its worst,
clutching him almost like a physical pain, a sudden
impulse drove him towards a church near which he
happened to be walking ; he quickened his steps,
entered, and, falling on his knees, prayed with all
his soul to be delivered from the trial, promising
that if God gave him light to see the truth, he would
for ever after devote himself to its defence." While
uttering this prayer, he felt that he was committing
himself to a distinct pledge which must colour his
whole life—that if his faith were restored to him,
his life must be concentrated to its service in no
ordinary way.

" I vowed," he said, "to consecrate my days to

the service of that truth which had given me peace."

Dr. Ozanam designed Frederic for the law; but, upon the completion of his studies, dreaded so much the risk to his faith and morals which would ensue from sending him to Paris that he placed him as clerk in an attorney's office in Lyons. Even at this age Frederic had commenced to take a strong interest in the philosophical discussions which had begun to agitate society. He was deeply grieved to observe the continuous spread of irreligion and scepticism. He saw how readily the weak-minded and the half-educated embraced the false theories of the philosophers, and he longed to establish a countervailing influence. He seems to have formed the idea thus early of an association of young men, who should be of mutual assistance and encouragement in religious exercises and good works. This idea was the germ from which the great Society of St. Vincent de Paul was destined to spring in future years.

We find him writing (1831) to a friend: "I felt that I had need of something solid to take hold of—something that I could take root in and cling to, in order to resist the torrent of doubt, and then my soul was filled with a great joy and a great consolation; for lo! it discovered by the sheer force of reason that this 'something was none other than that Catholicism which was first taught me by my mother, which was dear to my childhood, and so

often fed my mind and heart with its beautiful
hopes—Catholicism, with all its grandeurs and all
its delights! Shaken for a time with doubt, I felt
the invincible need to cling with all my might to
the pillar of the temple, were it even to crush me
in its fall; and lo! I find this same pillar supported
by science, luminous with the beams of wisdom, of
glory, and of beauty. I will take my stand by its
side, and there, stretching out my arm, I will point
to it as a beacon of deliverance to those who are
tossing on the sea of life. Happy shall I be if a
few friends come and rally round me. Then we
should unite our efforts, and create a work together;
others would join us, and perchance the day would
come when all mankind would be gathered together
beneath the same protecting shade. The preliminary
labours have already opened out to me the vast
perspective which I have unfolded to you, and over
which my imagination soars, transported with joy.
But it is a small thing to contemplate the career I
have to run; the thing is to start on the road, for
the hour is at hand. I dare say you will exclaim
at the audacity of this poor fellow, Ozanam. Just
as you like! But what is one to do? When an
idea has taken hold of you, and possesses your
whole mind for two years, are you free to with-
stand it? When a voice keeps continually crying
out to you—' Do this; *I so will it* '—can you bid it
be silent ?"

His letters about this period are in every way remarkable, especially when it is considered that they are the production of a youth of eighteen. They show him to have been possessed of a very high order of intellectual power, and of singular originality and force of character. Of such materials are made the great men of every age, men who are destined to leave their mark in history.

Dr. Ozanam considered that it was now time to give his son the opportunity of continuing his legal studies at Paris, as he had observed with satisfaction that Frederic possessed an earnestness of mind and a solidity of faith which would protect him against the dangers of the capital. He was entered as a student at the École de Droit, and we find him shortly after recording the bitterness of his disappointment. He found himself thrown among young men utterly destitute of religion, and with no respect for its ordinances. At the boarding-house where he lived he saw the same state of things—an utter indifference to religious observances. He found himself the only one who observed the Friday abstinence, and he was ridiculed and laughed at for his strictness. But he was not to be moved from his principles by such examples. He isolated himself altogether from s ociety, and sought his recreation in his books.

The old dream in which he had indulged while in Lyons, and which formed the scheme of his ambition, now returned. He grieved over the universal irreligion which he saw around him, and yearned to discover some means of combating the evil. Writing to a friend at this time, he said : " You know of old my longing to surround myself with young men feeling and thinking as I do; I know that there are many such, but they are scattered, and the task of gathering defenders under our flag is proverbially a difficult one."

In attending his lectures at the Sorbonne, he made the acquaintance of a few young men, Catholics like himself; the very differences which divided them from their fellow-students banded them the more firmly together, and formed the nucleus of a body which was destined in future years to leaven the infidelity of France. At this time the professors of the Sorbonne were, without exception, Voltairean, who lost no opportunity of casting ridicule upon the doctrines of Christianity, and endeavouring to oppose to them the latest discoveries in the then imperfectly developed sciences of geology, etc. Among these, the illustrious Professor Jouffroy, who held the Chair of Philosophy in 1832, had striven in his lectures to prove the impossibility of Revelation. Ozanam was indignant at the unsoundness and the one-sidedness of the arguments he adduced, and drew up a protest, which he forwarded to the Professor, who promised to reply to it. After the lapse of a fortnight, the Professor lightly alluded to the protest, and dismissed Ozanam's objections with a few contemptuous remarks.

Ozanam thereupon summoned together all the Catholics he could discover among the students, and drew up a formal protest, which was signed by fifteen names, and was read out publicly in the lecture-room before the whole body of students. " The Professor," Ozanam tells us, " hummed and hawed, confounded himself in apologies, declared that he never intended to attack Christianity in particular, which he held, on the contrary, in the highest veneration, and promised for the future not to wound the belief of any of his Catholic hearers."

A step so decisive and so bold as this could not fail to attract public attention. Numbers of Catholic young men now rallied around the little band, and evening meetings were organized for the discussion of subjects of common interest. By degrees these meetings grew into a kind of debating society; a large hall was hired by the generosity of a friend, and students of all shades of religious belief were invited to attend and to join in the debates. Ozanam was the recognized leader of the Catholic party, and even thus early distinguished himself by a simple but persuasive eloquence, which afterwards won him great renown as a Professor. A great many distinguished men attended the discussions, and among them Montalembert, Sainte-Beuve, Savigny, Ampère, Alfred de Vigny, and Considérant.

At this time the minds of men were in a ferment on religious questions, and on all sides the anti-Catholic party continued their attacks upon the Church. And this spirit of opposition was manifested so powerfully in the weekly discussions, that Ozanam found it necessary to draw more closely together the supporters of the Catholic cause. He accordingly proposed that the members should meet once a week at each others' houses, in order to concert together, before the great meeting, their scheme of action, and thus present to the enemy a more united front. At the same time he suggested that they might further utilize these private meetings by the performance of some good works.

His friends were much impressed with the value of the idea, and went off together to consult a M. Bailly, in whose judgment they had much confidence.

M. Bailly was the proprietor of a printing office, an intelligent man, and a fervent Catholic. Several young Catholic students boarded at his house, and he loved to assemble them around him, and to listen to their conversation upon subjects of historical and religious interest. The good man at once fell into their views, and offered them the use of his office in which to hold their private meetings.

The first meeting was held in May, 1833, and was presided over by M. Bailly himself. The objects of the " Conference," as it was then called, were at once laid down as being the service of God in the persons of the poor. "If you are in earnest," said M. Bailly, "about serving the poor as well as yourselves, you must not let it be a mere doling out of alms, bringing each your pittance of money or food; you must make it a medium of moral assistance; you must give them the alms of good advice." And this has been the keynote of the Society of St. Vincent de Paul ever since. The members show themselves to be in reality "brothers" to the poor whom they visit, and they are welcomed, not for the relief which they bring, but far more for their fraternal words of kindness, consolation, and advice.

Thus was established by eight young men that great Society which was destined to play so great a part in the preservation of Catholic faith and principles among the poor of France. Like the little grain of mustard-seed, it has now grown into a gigantic tree, whose branches extend in blessing over the whole earth.

But the foundation of the Society of St. Vincent de Paul is not the only claim which Frederic Ozanam has upon the gratitude of his fellow-countrymen. He saw with grief the rapid increase in the spirit of scepticism and unbelief among all classes of the French people. Every effort was made by the Press then, as in our own time and country, to throw discredit upon Catholics, and to

represent them as ignorant and unenlightened,
blindly holding on to the doctrines of an effete
religion through ignorance of the discoveries of
modern science. He saw clearly that this evil could
be encountered by the clergy alone, who were the
natural guardians of the deposit of Faith entrusted
to their keeping. But the pulpits in the various
churches of Paris offered no adequate defence to
the strong tide of infidelity. Bossuet and Fénélon,
Massillon and Bourdaloue, had no successors to their
talents, and the art of pulpit oratory appeared to
have almost died out in France.

Ozanam felt that the great need of the day was
an eloquent and enlightened preacher, well versed
in the most recent scientific discoveries, orator
enough to attract large audiences of the educated
classes, and able to contest successfully the theses
of the opponents of Christianity, and to fight them
with the same weapons of science which they themselves used.

He set himself to work to discover such a
preacher, and in due time his search was rewarded
with success. A young cleric, named Henri
Lacordaire, had been invited to deliver a course of
sermons to the pupils in the College St. Stanislas.
Ozanam was much struck with the impassioned
eloquence of this young preacher, and with the
variety of the stores of learning upon which he
drew for the illustration of his subjects. " There is

the man we want to confound Jouffroy and his school!" he exclaimed, after listening to one of these sermons.

He consulted with his friends, and resolved to submit his ideas to the Archbishop of Paris, Monseigneur de Quélen. The latter received him with much kindness, and Ozanam unfolded his views as to the necessity of meeting publicly the attacks which were constantly being made by the professors upon Christian truth. He ended by hinting respectfully his opinion that the Abbé Lacordaire would be a fitting man for the duty, on account of his powerful eloquence and extensive learning. He ended by pointing out that he had already attracted to hear him in the little college chapel some of the first names in France, such as Chateaubriand, Lamartine, Sainte - Beuve, Victor Hugo, and Berryer. The Archbishop agreed with him as to the necessity of in some way meeting the evil complained of, and promised to give the matter his consideration. The result was not what Ozanam had hoped for. The Archbishop probably feared that the appointment of so young a priest as the Abbé Lacordaire to so important a post as official defender of the Catholic cause might give rise to discontent among the older clergy. He therefore appointed seven of the best preachers of Paris of the old school to deliver a course of sermons upon Modern Philosophy. The course, however, did not have the effect of drawing an audience of the class desired, and Ozanam, by no means daunted, drew up an address to the Archbishop, which he got signed by two hundred of the most prominent Catholics of Paris, begging him to appoint Lacordaire to preach a course in Notre Dame.

It was long before the Archbishop yielded to so novel and unprecedented a request, but at length he did so, and the young Abbé Lacordaire commenced his series of conferences. It was a new era in the Catholic life in Paris. For, at the time we are speaking of, the philosophical fallacies of Voltaire and the modern scientists had made such progress, and had been so widely propagated by the French Press, that faith in Christianity had almost died out among the intellectual classes. The churches were but thinly attended, and that chiefly by women and children. Only a very few old men were to be found who had the courage to face the public ridicule which was directed against those who were weak enough to believe, and courageous enough to show outward tokens of their Faith. To be a Catholic was in those days looked upon in Paris as a mark of feebleness of intellect. Travellers in France at the present day will still recognize the existence of this feeling, notably in Paris and the larger commercial cities. But a vast and significant improvement soon took place. Large numbers of men were to be seen attending Mass and

the other services of the Church. During Lent and
Easter Week the clergy, whose duties at such seasons
were formerly merely nominal, found their numbers
all too small to administer the Sacraments to their
crowds of communicants. On all hands we have
the strongest proof that France recovered rapidly
from the deathly paralysis which seemed to have
fallen upon her.

And this recovery may be plainly traced to the
spiritual influence of the Conferences of the Abbé
Lacordaire and that of the work of Ozanam through
the Society of St. Vincent de Paul.

In 1837, Frederic Ozanam, having completed his
studies, took his degrees as a doctor of laws, and
began to practise as a barrister. Briefs came but
slowly to him, however, and he was obliged to eke
out his scanty income by reading law with some
pupils. The honest, outspoken manliness of his
character, while it had made him many enemies,
had also secured him the friendship of many distinguished men, even in the ranks of his opponents;
among these, the eminent philosopher, M. Cousin,
and the foremost champion of Catholic privileges in
the House of Peers, the accomplished young Count
de Montalembert.

Through their influence a professorship of Commercial Law was established at Lyons, and Ozanam
was appointed to the chair. The delicacy of this
act made a particularly strong impression on the

young man, as his father had just died, and he felt the necessity of being near to his mother, in order to assist her in bearing the heavy sorrow which had fallen upon them.

At Lyons Ozanam found that his friend, M. Chaurand, who had been with him one of the original members of the little conference in Paris, had established many branches of the Society of St. Vincent de Paul, and he gladly joined with him in the work, always, however, insisting on taking a subordinate position, and encouraging the brothers by his practical example. It is a beautiful mark of his perfect humility and unselfishness that at no period of his life would he allow himself the title of Founder of the Society. He always insisted that it had grown up out of the good feeling of the members on the one side, and the necessities of their brothers, the poor, upon the other.

In 1839, his mother, who had long been in failing health, died, and Ozanam felt the blow severely, for he was deeply attached to her. He felt himself now quite alone in the world, and had thoughts of following the example of his friend Lacordaire, who had gone to Rome in order to enter the great Order of St. Dominic.

His director, however, the good old Abbé Noirot, who had known Frederic from his childhood, and was thoroughly well acquainted with his character and capabilities, persuaded him that his true vocation was to remain in the world and to fight the battle of the Church from the rostrum.

M. Cousin now gave Ozanam a further proof of his friendship by offering him the position of pro-fessor at the Paris University, deeming the sphere of Lyons too narrow for his splendid abilities. He accepted, and was named Assistant-Professor in the Chair of Foreign Literature in the Sorbonne.

He was rejoiced, on returning to Paris, to find that the Society of St. Vincent de Paul had grown and flourished marvellously during his absence. More than 600 members assembled in the amphitheatre in which their meetings were held to welcome him; and these were not the whole of the members in Paris. " The majority," he says, "was composed of poor students, but set off, as it were, by a few persons of the very highest social position. I elbowed a Peer of France, a Councillor of State, several Generals and distinguished writers. I counted 25 pupils of the École Normale, out of 75 which it numbers; 10 of the Polytéchnique; one or two of the École d'État Major. That morning 150 members had gone up to the altar together. . . . We are now nearly 2,000 young men, enrolled in this peaceful crusade of charity. . . . Now, too, that an ever-increasing pauperism stands face to face, in rage and despera-tion, with a monied aristocracy, whose bowels of mercy have grown hardened, it is well that there should be found mediators who may prevent a collision, of which no man may foretell the horrible disasters; who will gain a hearing in both camps, and who will carry words of resignation to one and counsels of mercy to the other, giving everywhere the password, '*conciliation and love.*'" The estimate which he makes here of the value of the Society is very striking and very just. In France, Belgium, Germany, etc., it has acted as a powerful means of abolishing class prejudices, and reconciling the capitalist with the working man.

The position in which Ozanam now found himself, although a very distinguished one, was full of difficulty. For many years the Sorbonne had been the headquarters of the modern school of philosophy and rationalism. It was therefore no easy task for a youthful professor, fresh from the provinces, to call in question from such a rostrum the teaching of such men as Guizot, Villemain, and even his friend Cousin himself. But he nevertheless applied himself to the task with heroic boldness, for he knew that the battle which he was called upon to fight was that of God and Truth. At first his audience stared and wondered at the new views which were put before them, so different from what they had been accustomed to; but the narrow prejudices in their minds were soon swept away by the torrent of impassioned eloquence which flowed from their professor's lips. His arguments were irresistible, because they were strengthened by apparently inexhaustible stores of erudition, and by a logic which was faultless and inexorable. His boldness excited some surprise and much resentment among his fellow-professors; but his views were always expressed with so much mildness and courtesy of language, and were so well backed up by unanswerable proofs, that criticism was disarmed.

Among his colleagues was M. Lenormant, Assistant-Professor of History, who had succeeded M. Guizot. For the first three years of his professorship he had lectured as a sceptic, and in thorough accord with the spirit of the age; but he had been deeply impressed by the boldness with which M. Ozanam, a new professor, and a man of evidently great intellectual power and of clear logical mind, had upheld the principles of Christian philosophy, and had been led by him to examine more fully into the grounds of his own opposition to it. As a result of his inquiry, his mind was enlightened as to the truth and beauty of Christianity, and with manly boldness he resolved to publicly vindicate its teachings. The anti-Christian majority were furious; for Lenormant had hitherto been one of their foremost champions. MM. Michelet and Quinet, the leaders of the infidel party, stirred up the students to riotous demonstrations, which daily increased in intensity until the end of the term. Ozanam, who strongly sympathized with the difficulties which his colleague encountered, made it a point to attend personally all his lectures,

accompanied by a number of Catholic students of
his acquaintance, in order to encourage him in his
struggle, but the` opposition was too strong for
them.

The result is thus eloquently described by Miss
O'Meara:

" The recommencing of the lectures was the signal
for the renewal of the hostile demonstrations. M.
Lenormant's appearance was greeted with hisses, and
yells, and unseemly manifestations of dislike. He
began to speak, but his voice was drowned in hootings
and blasphemous cries. Ozanam, who was present,
unable to contain his indignation, leaped up beside
the lecturer, and stood for a moment surveying the
tumult with proud defiance. The courageous action
drew forth an instantaneous salvo of applause; but
Ozanam, with a scornful gesture, commanded silence,
and proceeded to tell the assembly what he thought
of their behaviour, and what value he set on their
plaudits. He spoke with a fiery vehemence which
startled all into attention; he adjured them, in the
name of liberty, which they so loudly invoked, to
respect liberty in others, and to allow every man the
freedom of his conscience. The effect of this harangue
was magical; the tumult ceased, and M. Lenormant
continued, or rather began, his lecture, and finished
it without interruption."

It says much for the high respect in which
Ozanam's character was held, even by his oppo-

nents, that shortly after this defiance of the ruling spirit of the University, he was chosen to succeed to the Chair of Foreign Literature in the Sorbonne on the death of M. Fauriel, although at the time only thirty-two years of age. For many years he had been working steadily at his duties, giving the day to his lectures, the evening to the meetings of the Conferences of St. Vincent de Paul. But his health, which had never been very robust, gradually broke down under his continued exertions, and in 1847 he was ordered by his physician to pass the winter in Rome. He has left us in his works a record of his impressions of the Eternal City, which in purity of language and elevation of thought compares favourably with any-thing in the French language. In the autumn of 1847 he returned to Paris, and resumed his lectures at the Sorbonne with his old energy, and with recruited health. He had need of all his energy and strength now, for ample calls were about to be made on both.

On February 24, 1848, the revolution broke out. It was a great moral earthquake which overthrew all the foundations of society. Ozanam did his duty as a citizen ; he enrolled himself in the National Guard, and prepared, if necessary, to fight for the cause of order. At the elections he was invited to come forward as a candidate for Lyons, but he firmly refused, on the ground of ill-health. He felt that he could benefit his country more by his writings in the Press than by speeches in the Assemblée Nationale.

On April 13, in conjunction with Père Lacordaire, he started a newspaper, entitled the *Ère Nouvelle*, with the object of welding together the Catholic party and the working-classes, and advocating the principles of a Christian democracy. Thus, the founders thought, might be formed a solid foundation upon which the Republic might rest secure—that Republic of order which, in the minds of these intrepid soldiers of the Church, was now the only hope of good government in France. But the new paper had but a short existence; it made many enemies in each of the camps which it tried to unite. Accordingly it was sorrowfully abandoned after a few weeks, and its promoters turned their attention to the absorbing political events of the day.

The revolution increased in intensity. Barricades were erected in the streets of Paris, and General Cavaignac was organizing his troops and preparing to meet force by force. At this juncture Ozanam was destined to play an important part in a tragedy which will always be memorable in the history of France.

One day, when he was posted on guard, with M. Bailly and another friend in the Rue Madame, he suggested that the Archbishop of Paris, who was so popular with the people, might be able to put an end to the disastrous civil war if he would appear on the barricades, and exhort the insurgents to surrender, on the promise of a free pardon for the past. The friends agreed, and at once sallied off to the residence of the Archbishop, and submitted their idea to him. To their great surprise he quietly remarked: " I have been pursued by the same idea since yesterday; but how can it be done ?"

Ozanam explained the project they had formed, and the good Archbishop, having vested himself in his purple soutane and wearing his archiepiscopal cross, accompanied them to the quarters of General Cavaignac. The latter explained to the Archbishop the dangerous nature of his attempt, and endeavoured to dissuade him from the enterprise. Finding, however, that he was determined to carry it out, he entrusted to his care a proclamation to the insurgents, offering them a free pardon if they would lay down their arms.

Thus armed, the saintly Archbishop, with a solemn placidity which deeply affected the bystanders, returned home, made his confession, left a few written instructions concerning business matters, and proceeded to the barricade in the Faubourg St. Antoine, accompanied by his two Vicars-General, Ozanam and some members of the Conference of St. Vincent de Paul. When they arrived on the Place de la Bastille, the Archbishop mounted on the barricade, holding the proclamation in his hand. From an open window a shot was fired at this moment, and Archbishop Affré fell back mortally wounded. His last word were, " May my blood be the last shed!" And his prayer was heard ; for the *émeute* came to an end at once.

This dreadful tragedy affected Ozanam very deeply; for he felt that he had been unwittingly the instrument of Providence in winning a palm of glorious martyrdom for the Archbishop.

From this time forward his health rapidly failed him, and he was compelled constantly to seek rest and relaxation from his duties. In 1851 he was induced by a scientific friend to pay a visit to London, to see the wonders of the Great Exhibition. He had never visited England before, and was much struck with the evidences of vast material wealth which met him upon every side. But they suggested very grave reflections. " It looks to me," he said, " like a seal of reprobation on these riches that they do not serve to ameliorate the lot of humanity—the lot, that is, of the greater number—and that the most opulent city in the world is also that which treats its poor most harshly. . . . The English cannot prevent mendicity from penetrating into London—they tolerate it—and I give them credit for doing so ; but why, then, do they insult so derisively the mendicity of Catholic countries ? Never in the streets of Rome did I see anything approaching to these women in rags, who hold out their hands to you as you pass along the Strand—to those little girls one sees, in a frock tattered up to their waist, with their naked feet in the cold black mud."

On his return to France his health continued to decline; but he still clung manfully to his duties at the Sorbonne, as of old.

At last, in 1852, he was struck down by a serious attack of pleurisy, which confined him to his bed for many weeks. He was still in this condition when a rumour reached him that ungenerous remarks had been made as to his neglect of his duties at the Sorbonne, which had been ascribed to love of ease. He was stung to the quick by the news.

"I will show them it is not true; I will do honour to my profession!" he cried.

And notwithstanding the entreaties of his wife and of his brother, who was attending him, he rose and drove to the Sorbonne. He found in the lecture-room a crowd of students, who started when they beheld his pale face, and his thin, attenuated frame worn out by suffering. Amid repeated rounds of applause he ascended the rostrum, and delivered a lecture which surpassed in eloquence and grace even those of his palmiest days. At its conclusion the applause was loud and long; but his friends saw sorrowfully at what cost he had delivered it. It was a final and a fatal effort, and he returned to his house like a dying man.

By the advice of his physician he was moved to the Pyrenees, where his health recovered sufficiently to allow of his visiting a few of the coast towns, and even making a short excursion into Spain. He then journeyed by short stages to Italy, where the balmy air seemed to do him much good at first; and for a time the expiring flame of life flickered with something like its old brilliancy. But he knew that his end was approaching, and he besought Almighty God for the last grace of being allowed to die in his own loved France, among the people whom he loved, and for whose benefit he had worked so long. His prayer was heard, and he was able to return by sea to Marseilles. He wished to proceed to Paris, in order that he might yield up his soul in the city which had been the scene of his labours, but he was already too much exhausted with the fatigue of his long journey.

After receiving the last Sacraments with much devotion, he gave up his soul to God on the Feast of the Nativity of our Lady, September 8, 1853.

His whole life was an example of what great things a man of good heart and will can do. Few men are endowed with the brilliant talents of Frederic Ozanam; but his charity to all men, and his love of the poor, can be imitated, and should be the model of all members of the Society of St. Vincent de Paul.

CHAPTER II

THE ESTABLISHMENT OF THE SOCIETY OF
ST. VINCENT DE PAUL IN ENGLAND

CHAPTER II

WHEN Ozanam returned from Lyons to Paris and commenced his lectures at the Sorbonne, he was gratified to see them attended by many young men of various nationalities. He gladly made the acquaintance of these, and persuaded some of them to join the Conference of St. Vincent de Paul at St. Étienne du Mont. Among these was a young Englishman named George Jonas Wigley, a student at the École des Beaux Arts, and another, an American. Ozanam took special interest in these, and thoroughly impressed them with his conviction that a new spirit of revolt against Religion and Law had arisen, and was destined to uproot the foundations upon which social order was based. Religion was the only barrier to some great social upheaval, which would surely come sooner or later. There were signs of its rapid approach in France, and he believed that all the chief industrial nations would be affected by it, especially England, America, and Belgium. He felt strongly that the spirit of class hatred, of the revolt of Labour against Capital, could only be combated

by a revival of Religion, and by the personal visits
to the poor at their own homes by educated Catholics,
who would fraternize with the workmen and advise
them. This, he said, was the principal object of the
Conferences of St. Vincent de Paul, and their work
had already been very effective in Paris and Lyons.
Hearing that Wigley was contributing some articles
to the only Catholic newspaper in London, the
Tablet, and that the Editor, Mr. Frederick Lucas,
was a friend of his, Ozanam advised Wigley to
write an account of the objects of the Conferences
of St. Vincent de Paul in France, and of the beneficial effects of their work among the poor. This
Wigley did, and Mr. Lucas took up the cause
warmly, and advocated the establishment of the
Society in London. Ozanam was delighted with
the news, and supplied Wigley with numbers of
interesting statistics and instances of what had been
done in France. Through Wigley he invited Lucas
to act as Founder and first President of the Society
in London. This honour, however, was declined by
Lucas, but he succeeded in gaining the approval of
the Vicar-General of the diocese, and of Bishop
Griffiths. A number of influential Catholics were
induced to form a committee for the purpose, among
whom was Mr. Pagliano, the proprietor of the
Sablonière Hotel in Leicester Square. There the
first Conference used to meet weekly, Mr. Pagliano
acting as temporary President. Wigley translated

the rules, etc., into English, and, at Ozanam's
request, returned to London and helped the new
Conference to take the necessary steps for the organization of the Society and its affiliation to that of
Paris. New ideas are slow to take root in England.
English Catholics in the middle of last century were
especially timid and apprehensive of the effects of
introducing new works of charity by Catholics upon
their Protestant fellow-countrymen. It was too soon
after Catholic emancipation from the slavery of the
Penal Laws to risk the revival of the " No Popery "
cries in the streets. And therefore the progress of
the infant Society was very slow. But Conferences
were gradually started in many of the London
missions, and were joined by many members, who
recognized the practical value of the work.

In impressing upon Wigley the importance of
introducing the Society into England, Ozanam used
some strange arguments. He said that England had
done a very great wrong to France in the eighteenth
century, and owed her reparation for it. He said
that the first French Revolution had been initiated
and fomented by English Freemasons who had
established the Order in Paris, and that the leaders
of the Revolution in France were all members of
the Order, the headquarters of which were in
London, while its principles were opposed to Christianity and to the authority of the State. Also that
the theories of the " Rights of Man," which had

been put forward by English philosophers, had sown the seeds of Socialism among the working classes in France, and had fomented the spirit of revolution and class hatred. He predicted that the inevitable result would be a war of Labour against Capital, the outcome of which would be a great commercial and social crisis, from which England and America would suffer more than France. It was fitting, therefore, he said, that Catholic France should repay the evil which England had done her by the good service which the Society of St. Vincent de Paul would render her by providing an antidote of charity and love of the poor against irreligion and anarchy.

A prominent quality in Ozanam's character was his desire to see theories illustrated by facts. He felt that it was not enough to preach a doctrine; we must also practise it if we wish to get men to accept it. Thus we find him writing, in March, 1833, to his friend, Ernest Falconnet:

" You knew before I left Lyons what was the object of my ambition. You know that I hoped to form a reunion of friends working together at the building up of scientific knowledge under the standard of Catholic Faith. This idea remained for a long time latent, until a friend introduced me to a small literary society, the last remains of the old Committee of Research, but the unscientific methods of which left but little scope for philosophic and serious investigations. The average attendance at these meet-

ings was fifteen, and it was scarcely dared to intro-
duce the higher questions of the future or of the
past for consideration. Now the Society numbers
sixty, and includes men of some note, students of
art, philosophy, political economy, but mostly of
historical subjects, and even two or three poets."

Some of these young men were destined to make
names for themselves in the world. Among those
he mentions we find Montalembert, Lacordaire,
Ampère, Alfred de Vigny, Sainte-Beuve, de Mérode,
Lherminier, Victor Considérant, etc.

On January 29, 1844, several Catholics met at the
Sablonière Hotel—viz., Pagliano, Frederick Lucas
(founder and editor of the *Tablet*), George J. Wigley,
William Amherst, George Blount, Bosanquet, Robert
Barnewall, Martial Thompson, Wright, Carew,
James Floris, John Rogers Herbert (later a Royal
Academician). It was resolved " that it was advis-
able that an institution should be formed on the
basis of the Society of St. Vincent de Paul, established
in France, for London and its vicinity."

On February 12 it was resolved to form the
" Brotherhood of St. Vincent de Paul." This title
was altered to that of the " Society of St. Vincent de
Paul," on aggregation by the Council-General of the
Society in Paris.

Brother Frederick Lucas, who, by articles in the
Tablet, had done much to bring about this movement,
was elected President, but he declined. Brother

Pagliano was then elected, and continued President till 1852.

During this period the " Clifton Tracts," in refutation of violent anti-Catholic attacks in consequence of the establishment of the Hierachy in 1850, were published by the " Brotherhood of St. Vincent de Paul." Brother J. Spencer Northcote (at that time a layman, and afterwards Provost of the Chapter of the Diocese of Birmingham) was editor.

On the resignation of the Presidency by Brother Pagliano in 1852, Brother George Blount, at the age of thirty-three, was elected on January 16, and continued President till his death, at eighty years of age, on January 18, 1899, a period of forty-seven years. He lived to see the Society raised from a few Conferences, on his accession to the Presidency, to 170 Conferences, with a total of 3,057 members, on December 31, 1898.

A subscription was set on foot to honour his memory by some Work of Patronage for Boys, which was his favourite work.

A freehold house and grounds were purchased, and the " George Blount Home for Working Boys " was opened at 31, Mitcham Lane, Streatham, London. Accommodation is there provided for twenty boys between the ages of fourteen and eighteen, who are either orphans or whose homes are objectionable, and who have daily employment. The work is carried on successfully by the Patronage

Committee, with the support of the Conferences and members of the Society throughout England.

On Brother George Blount's death, Brother the Marquess of Ripon was elected President, and on his death, July 9, 1909, was succeeded by Brother Sir John Knill, Bart.

Following Brother Ozanam's maxim that "no good work is foreign to the Society," the English Conferences started works of charity of many kinds in every parish in which they were established. In co-operation with the parish priest, who was generally chaplain to the Conference, they established ladies' societies for the care of cases of women and children outside the scope of the Society. One of the first works to be established was that of the Catholic Shoeblack Brigade for the employment of poor boys, which was followed by the establishment of the Working Boys' Home and the Patronage Committee. The next work founded by the Society was the St. Vincent's Home for Destitute Boys at Hammersmith. This was a separate work, managed by a committee of members of the London Council, of which Brother George Blount was President. After being carried on for fifteen years, it was handed over to the care of Father Lord Archibald Douglas. It is now carried on by the "Crusade of Rescue for Destitute Catholic Children," established by the late Cardinal Vaughan, and which supports nearly one thousand boys and girls. Numbers of these are sent every year to Canada, where their future is fully provided for.

In 1859, the year of the terrible war which robbed the Church of its patrimony and deprived the Holy Father of the necessary means for carrying on the rule of the Universal Church, Cardinal Wiseman appealed to the London Council to support a movement initiated by Brother Wigley for the revival of the ancient subsidy paid to the Holy See by our Saxon forefathers. This was called " Peter's Pence." His Eminence also asked that the Society should establish a cheap newspaper accessible to the poor, which should publish the truth concerning the war which was being waged by Victor Emmanuel, Cavour, and Garibaldi against the Church. In both cases the London Council found itself unable by the rules of the Society to undertake the responsibilities proposed, but collateral committees were formed by which they were carried out. A penny newspaper was established, named the *Universe*, and which worked in conjunction with M. Louis Veuillot, the proprietor of *L'Univers* of Paris. At the request of Cardinal Wiseman, the writer acted as first editor and Brother Wigley as foreign colleague.

In like manner the Peter's Pence Association was formed of members of the Society, George Wigley being Hon. Secretary, Lords Feilding and Campden (afterwards Earls of Denbigh and Gainsborough) and myself as Hon. Treasurers.

CHAPTER III

THE DEVELOPMENT OF THE SOCIETY OF
ST. VINCENT DE PAUL THROUGHOUT THE WORLD

CHAPTER III

THE aims and objects of the Society of St. Vincent
de Paul cannot be better set forth than in the following preface to the official Report of the Superior
Council of England for 1912:

"The Society of St. Vincent de Paul is a Society
of men in all countries associated together for mutual
encouragement in the practice of a Christian life.
By taking an active part, however small, in works of
mercy, they hope to make progress in piety, and
with this object they try to be the friends of the
poor, visiting and relieving them in distress, in-
structing them in religion, visiting workhouses,
hospitals, and similar institutions, distributing
wholesome reading, conducting Penny Banks and
Libraries, and giving such kinds of help as may be
most required. Mindful of their holy Patron's care
for the young, they take a great interest in boys, and
they try to benefit them by assisting in the conduct
of their clubs, seeing that they attend Catholic

38

Schools, obtaining suitable situations for them when they leave school, and supervising their attendance at Mass and Catechism. Many other works are undertaken by the Society, varying according to circumstances, but the above are universally needed and belong to its general practice. It is a primary rule that no work of charity is foreign to the Society.

"Members are either Active or Honorary. An Active Member need not do more than attend the weekly Conference Meeting, at which there is a voluntary and strictly secret collection, and visit one poor family. As this need not occupy much more than an hour a week, no great demand is made upon his time, while he may easily find full employment for any amount of leisure and charitable zeal. The Society was founded by young men, and these are invited earnestly to become Active Members, assuring them of the brotherly welcome with which they will be received, and the speedy reward they will win in the gratitude of the poor.

" Honorary Members incur no obligation but the contribution of a fixed sum, annually or otherwise, to the Society's funds, the amount being optional, and no minimum being fixed ; they are entitled to attend all general meetings, retreats, etc., and to participate in the Society's prayers and good works, and they add very much to its strength.

" All men are eligible as Members provided they

4

are in a position to contribute anything, however small, to the Society's funds, and are so far practising their religion that they may be expected to edify their fellow-members and be edified by them.

"There are 308 Conferences in England, which assemble at a stated time each week, and at which the brothers meet to join in common prayers and spiritual reading, to discuss the visiting and other works in progress, and to promote the objects of the Society. Men desiring to join the Society should communicate in writing with the local President, or with the Secretary of the Superior Council, from whom copies of the rules, reports, and all information can be obtained. Where no Conference exists, any eligible men may he enrolled as Corresponding members, and will so participate in the works and benefits of the Society.

"Ladies cannot be members, but by subscribing an annual amount, however small, they can be enrolled as 'Benefactresses,' and as such are enabled to obtain special Indulgences; and they may be of great assistance to the Society, either individually or in associations, by entering into communication with it, undertaking to visit cases more suitable to them, dispensing the Society's relief to such cases, and helping to provide clothing, sick relief, bedding, or employment for the poor, or distributing literature.

"The Society is entirely non-political, but is open

to co-operate with any charitable societies, whether Catholic or not, for the better care of the poor.

" The Rule of the Society was duly submitted to and approved by the Holy See, which in token of approbation has at various times enriched the work with ample Indulgences, particulars of which will be found in the Rule Books and cards of the Society. The present Holy Father deigned thus to address the President-General and some other members of the Society, whom he received in private audience on May 11, 1904 :

"'BELOVED SONS,—I wish to thank you for all the good you are doing. Yes, assuredly, I know your Society. I saw it at work at Mantua, and in Venice, where it was rendering invaluable services to the poor by distributing alms, but still more so by bringing them spiritual aid. How many families have been saved through its intervention ! but above all, how many young men have been led back to the right path by it ! The Society of St. Vincent de Paul is a work of apostleship for good, while there are others which are, at the present day, works of apostleship for evil. Continue, therefore, to exercise charity in the way you are doing ; you will find in it peace for your soul, and (he added smiling) when one has done some good in the day, he rests more peacefully at night. Your Society is the work needed for the present times. I will encourage and bless it.' "

The organization of the Society is as follows:

The General Council of the Society is situated in Paris. It has jurisdiction over the Superior Councils which are established in every country.

The Superior Councils have jurisdiction over the various Councils presiding over the Conferences in the districts of the country allotted to them. These are called Central Councils, and have control over what are called Particular Councils serving sub-divisions of their district.

An example of the organization of the Society in England will best illustrate its methods:

The Superior Council of England has under it six Central Councils, eighteen Particular Councils, and 308 Conferences.

These Councils are situated respectively at Birmingham, Bristol, Cardiff, Liverpool, Manchester, and Newcastle-on-Tyne.

Under these Central Councils there are Particular Councils at London, Liverpool, Preston, Manchester, Blackburn, Burnley, Bury, Oldham, Rochdale, New-castle, Jarrow, Durham, Bradford, Leeds, Plymouth, Portsmouth, and Sheffield. There are, in addition, fifty-three isolated Conferences situated in country towns not yet grouped under Particular Councils.

The total number of active and honorary members attached to the 308 Conferences of the Society in England in 1912 is given as 5,818. The total number of visits paid by them to poor families in

1912 is stated as 160,526. In addition, there were 45 orphans partly or wholly supported; 6,149 boys under the care of Patronage Committees; 2,585 boys attending Sunday-schools; and 3,195 adults attending Clubs and Evening Schools.

Finally, the net receipts of the Conferences in England in 1912 were £13,575 3s. 9d., and the actual expenditure, £12,461 7s. 2d.

The Reports of the Conferences throughout the country to their respective Councils show a remarkable record of the variety of good works carried out by the brothers in addition to their normal work of visiting the poor at their own homes as friends. In nearly every parish some member of the Conference registers the attendance of boys at Mass, and afterwards teaches in the Sunday-schools. Hence they keep in friendly relations with the families of the children. Other members of the Conference attend Police Courts, Workhouses, etc., to see that Catholic children are suitably provided for in respect to religious matters.

Others, again, organize Boys' Clubs for Cricket and Football, Boys' Brigades, Boy Scouts, etc. They also manage Young Men's Clubs, Evening Schools for adults, etc.

Some Conferences support, wholly or in part, destitute boys in orphanages, supplying them with clothing, etc. One Conference reports that one of the poor boys under their charge won a scholarship, and the Conference provided him with a complete outfit to go to college.

The most striking point in all the reports of Conferences with respect to their patronage works is the prevailing anxiety shown by them to look after the boy at the most critical period of his life, when he leaves the protection of school and home, and is exposed to the demoralizing influence of other boys of his own age, who have had no religious and moral training, and whose sole idea of life is to seek for material pleasures and amusements.

This is the most important of all works of the Society, for it is training the men of the next generation, who will in turn influence succeeding generations for good or ill.

Many Conferences allude to the desirability of apprenticing boys to trades which will provide a future for them, but all lament the double barriers which prevent their action. These are, first, the payment of the apprenticeship fee, and the helping to support the boy until such time as he can earn sufficient wages ; and the next is the refusal of the Trades Union to allow more than a certain number of boys to be apprenticed except in proportion to the men employed.

In Ireland there is a Superior Council in Dublin, with Central Councils at Derry with 15 Conferences; Kilmore with 5 Conferences; and Down and Connor with 58 Conferences.

There are Particular Councils at Dublin with 32 Conferences; Belfast with 20 Conferences; Cork with 4 Conferences; Derry with 5 Conferences; Limerick with 4 Conferences; and Waterford with 4 Conferences. In addition there are 144 isolated Conferences in various districts. The total number of Conferences in Ireland is 210, having 4,601 active and honorary members.

In Scotland there is a Superior Council of Edinburgh and 1 Particular Council with 27 Conferences and 329 active and 46 honorary members. In Glasgow there is a Superior Council with 67 Conferences and 958 members. There is also the Central Council of Galloway with 9 Conferences and 123 active and honorary members.

In France itself there are 1,522 Conferences, with a membership of 24,300 brothers.

In Belgium there are 1,188 Conferences with 23,689 brothers.

In Italy there are 342 Conferences, with 6,579 brothers.

Spain has 551 Conferences with 14,921 members.

Switzerland 72 Conferences and 2,321 members.

In the Dominions overseas of the British Empire, there are also 337 Conferences with a membership of 11,804 active and honorary brothers.

In India there is at Bombay the Central Council of Western India with 1 Particular Council and 18 Conferences with 499 active and honorary members.   There are also Conferences at Calcutta, Rangoon, Ceylon, Singapore, Hong-Kong, Shanghai, Gibraltar, and Malta.

In Canada there is a Superior Council with 2 Central and 13 Particular Councils, and 157 Conferences with 7,690 active and honorary members. These Conferences are situated in all the provinces and cities of the Dominion.

In British Guiana there is a Particular Council and 3 Conferences, English and Portuguese.   There are also Conferences in Jamaica, Trinidad, Santa Lucia, and Haiti.

There is a Superior Council of Australasia, comprising Australia, New Zealand, and Tasmania; it includes 2 Central and 9 Particular Councils; there are 175 Conferences with 3,242 active and honorary members.   There are Central Councils in New South Wales and Melbourne, and Particular Councils at Melbourne, Sydney, Bendigo, Adelaide, Brisbane, Charters Towers, Christchurch, Wellington, Auckland, etc.

In Africa there is a Central Council of the Western Province of Cape Colony, with 6 Conferences; a Central Council at Port Elizabeth with 7 Conferences.   There are also Conferences at Durban, Pietermaritzburg, Johannesburg, and Kimberley.

In the United States the first Conference of the Society of St. Vincent de Paul was established in 1845 at St. Louis, Missouri, and in New York in 1846. The Society and its objects were enthusiastically taken up by the practical American people, and it is now thoroughly organized in all the States. The statistics for 1910 show that there were 730 Conferences, with 12,062 active and honorary members. In that year there were 24,742 families visited, and 233,044 visits paid to them, while 2,949 situations were found for members of the families. The amount expended in charity, etc., during the year was $387,849.

Among the various works taken up or supervised by the Conferences in the United States may be mentioned the support of Orphans, Homes for homeless lads, or for those employed in works, Boys' Clubs, visits paid to Hospitals and Prisons, Sailors' Homes, Employment Registers, the work known as that of St. Francis Regis for supplying the certificates required by the French Law for marriages, etc.

The Society of St. Vincent de Paul is entirely a lay organization. The Conferences are established in the parishes with the consent of, and for the assistance of, the parish priest, who generally acts as chaplain. The Rules are simple and practical, and are distinguished by a truly democratic simplicity. The President of the Conference is elected by the members and confirmed by the Council of the town where it is situated. These local Councils consist of the Presidents, Secretaries, and Treasurers of the various Conferences within their jurisdiction. These local

Councils, again, are grouped into Provincial Councils, which are governed by a Superior Council, which generally includes all those in a nation or province.

The Council-General of the Society meets in Paris, and is reported to by all the Superior Councils throughout the world.

The constitution of the Society is essentially democratic; the President is only *primus inter pares*, all the members of the Conference, whether they be peers, shopkeepers, or workmen, are equal. No political discussion is permitted at the meetings of the Conference. There is another remarkable rule which marks it off from all other charitable societies, there are no paid officers in the Society—all services are gratuitous, and the meetings of most Conferences are held in the schoolrooms of the church. Thus the whole income of the Society goes to the poor direct, for the brothers carry it to their charges on the weekly visits which they pay to them. It may be added, as an example, that the meetings of the Superior Council of England are held in the crypt of one of the London churches. There is a strange contrast shown between the balance sheet of the Society of St. Vincent de Paul and those of the great majority of charitable associations, which generally show an expenditure of about one-third of the total subscriptions in the costs of administration.

Another characteristic of the Society is the spirit of Catholic modesty and self-effacement which was enjoined on its members by Ozanam. He was intensely opposed to ostentation, and did not approve of the brothers wearing any distinctive dress or badge, or even of their taking part officially as a body in any public ceremony or procession. But he strongly recommended the brothers to mingle in the ranks of any religious processions of the people in private dress, and thus to encourage the devotion of the poor whom they visit.

It would seem that the Society of St. Vincent de Paul, with its unassuming and practical work and its absence of any kind of self-advertisement, should be a very attractive one to Englishmen, in whom the spirit of philanthropy is so general. But the work does not appear to be sufficiently known or understood, or the number of its members would be greater and its finances strengthened. Nevertheless we see frequently in Catholic newspapers piteous complaints of recent converts that they cannot find sufficient outlets in their parishes for their fervent zeal. And yet there is a Conference of the Society in every parish, at the weekly meetings of which a few unobtrusive members attend and study the needs of the poor, who, as our Lord said, "are always with us."

CHAPTER IV

THE FUTURE OF THE SOCIETY

CHAPTER IV

THE FUTURE OF THE SOCIETY

THE Society of St. Vincent de Paul is destined to play an important part in the future of the Catholic Church in England. For it is a living contradiction to the falsehoods about Catholics, which have been repeated *ad nauseam* by historians during the past three hundred years. Our Church has been represented as the enemy of civilization and of liberty, and Catholics generally as a superstitious, uneducated, and weak-minded class. Less than a century has passed since Catholics gained their rights as citizens. Many of us must remember the stigma under which in youth we laboured as Catholics. Most of the professions were closed against us, as well as all the great English Universities. Everything we did was misrepresented and distorted in the public Press; monks and nuns were shamefully vilified and accused of dark and mysterious outrages in their convents. And all these lies were believed against us by the Protestant public.

But a great change has taken place in public opinion during the past fifty years. It has been

found that, after all, Catholics are not the evil-dis-
posed people they were thought to be, and that they
are even capable of doing some good. And this
change has been partly brought about by the Society
of St. Vincent de Paul. For although it does not
advertise its good works as Protestant societies do,
nor spend one-third of its income in salaries (or
even any of it), the example of its brothers in visiting
and relieving the poor, and the self-sacrifice which
this entails, is gradually getting known throughout
the country.

Sir Arthur Helps said that there is no better
training for life than the discipline of the playground
of a public school, and he was right. But for a study
of human life and character there is no better school
than a Conference of St. Vincent de Paul. In the
visits which a brother pays to his cases, what
dramas and even tragedies of real life he meets with !
What comedies and even farces, caused by ignorance
and inexperience ! What touching examples of
charity and self-sacrifice among the very poorest in
helping one another ! Believe me, we have more to
learn from the cases we visit than we can teach
them !

To compare the Society of St. Vincent de Paul in
1844, when it was established in England, with
that of 1913 is like comparing the Thames at its
source among the hills, where a man can jump
across it, with the great stream at London Bridge.

From being a small and insignificant Society it has
grown to be a mighty influence for good throughout
the world.   It might well say with the Roman poet :

"Quæ regio in terris, nostri non plena laboris !"

But it would not accord with the modest spirit of
the Society to make such a boast.

Ozanam's prophecy that the Society would prove
an antidote to the poison of Socialism is likely to be
verified in England in such districts as are influenced
by the Conferences.   In founding the Society he
tried to realize a dream of his youth ; he saw that
in his own country men were divided into two cate-
gories—the rich and landed gentry, and the working
classes.   The rich looked down on the poor as being
ignorant and uncultivated slaves, while the poor
regarded the rich as a class of men living upon the
fruits of the toil of the working classes.   Ozanam
recognized that there was a modicum of truth in
both views.   He knew that one of the causes of the
first French Revolution had been the well-known
indifference shown by the landowners of France to
the welfare of the people who cultivated their lands
and created their large revenues, and whom they
treated as serfs.   He knew that in the sight of God
all men, whether Kings or peasants, masters or
servants, were equal, and that the Church had
always treated them as such.   The sons of peasants
had become Bishops and Popes ; and many Saints

canonized by her were of the same extraction. He knew that the monastic life was the realization of an ideal republic, where the Abbot, perhaps the son of a peasant, was often the ruler of a community which counted among its numbers Princes and members of the highest families in the land. And yet he was only *primus inter pares*. "Liberty, Equality, and Fraternity," for which the revolutionaries raved hypocritically, were only to be found in perfection within the walls of a monastery.

In his lectures at the Sorbonne he had always argued that history proved that the Church had ever been the true promoter of civilization and culture and the protector of the poor. It was necessary that this fact should be brought home to the hearts of the people, and both he and his friend Lacordaire impressed this upon their hearers in their lectures and sermons. But the poor and the workmen did not frequent either the Sorbonne or the Notre Dame, and they only knew of either by the travesties which were published in the infidel papers, which alone they read.

Ozanam felt that the only way to reach the minds and hearts of the working classes must be by laymen. The anti-clerical feeling in Paris was very strong, and a priest would not be listened to. And it was for this reason that he established the Conferences of St. Vincent de Paul.

He determined that the Conference should consist

of laymen, not priests; not a confraternity, but a meeting of friends united unassumingly to do good to the poor, to visit, advise, and relieve them, thus performing the spiritual and corporal works of mercy. He was totally opposed to the Society advertising itself in any way, either by badge or by publishing lists of subscriptions.

When Ozanam spoke to the men of Paris in praise of the Church, and in commendation of her power to heal the evils of Society, it was said to him : " If you speak of the past, what you say is true. Christianity did do wonders, but now it is played out. What works are you doing to prove your Faith, and to make us respect and believe it ?" Ozanam felt the full force of the retort, and resolved to remove further occasion for it. He said to his Catholic friends: "We must bestir ourselves and make our actions agree with our Faith. Let us, therefore, turn to the assistance of the needy, and so put our faith under the protection of charity."

In this you have the true motto of the Society of St. Vincent de Paul—Faith, under the protection of Charity. The Society was created to be a vindication of the Church by the exercise of charity in its widest sense, charity for mind, charity for heart, charity for the body, charity for the whole man— full and perfect service to our neighbour by charity of the spirit. The Society was intended to be a proof of the healing power of Christianity, a testimony before men of the truth and beneficence of the Church. Is this idea too ambitious ? Ozanam would have replied that no one can measure the power of charity, for it appeals to the human heart as nothing else can. Force may compel an unwilling submission, but the loving counsel of a friend wins the heart and keeps it.

As the good work done by the Society becomes better known and appreciated, the Conferences must increase in number, and attract to themselves numbers of active and honorary members, especially of young men. The weekly meetings of the Conferences are short and business-like, the subscriptions are placed secretly in a bag like any ordinary collection in church, nobody knows what his neighbour has given. The case which is given to the brother to visit will deeply interest him, the employment of the father, his wages, his health, the attendance of the children at Mass and Sunday-schools, their employment when they leave school, and their supervision ; all of these are matters of human interest, and subjects of special study.

Some persons have objected to join or to subscribe to the Conferences of St. Vincent de Paul upon principle. They said that they thought that almsgiving to the poor was very demoralizing and pauperizing, that it was humiliating to the poor, and destructive of their manly self-respect and independence. But does not everything depend upon the way the help is offered? No brother of the Society of St. Vincent de Paul could confirm such a theory from his personal experience. They are not relieving officers; they visit the families as friends and sympathizers, anxious to know how they can help the family—by advice as to the children, by getting hospital tickets when required, by arranging quarrels and family disputes, by getting the children employment when they leave school, or by suitable introductions. They do not go to patronize but to fraternize ; they sit down and talk familiarly with the family, showing that they come as friends and by no means as patrons. Hence it comes that the brother is always a welcome visitor. The material relief is always a subsidiary matter, it is the friendly interest and advice which is valued.

The Society already comprises a great number of works of charity of every description, but it is always ready to join in any work which may benefit the poor ; for it has adopted literally Ozanam's noble motto : " No good work is foreign to the Society." Future generations will inevitably witness a great development, not only in the number of Conferences, but also in that of the brothers.

CHAPTER V

THE CENTENARY CELEBRATIONS IN PARIS AND MANCHESTER

CHAPTER V

A CENTENARY Celebration in the honour of Frederic
Ozanam was solemnly held at Paris. It was an
international meeting, and was attended by representatives of the Conferences of the Society from all
parts of the world. The 5,000 members of the
Society in Paris were joined by 1,356 from the
provinces and abroad. Cardinal Vincent Vannutelli,
who was sent by the Holy Father as Papal Legate to
attend the Centenary, arrived at Paris on April 23,
1913, accompanied by his suite. On the same day
he received the President and the members of the
Council-General of the Society, and expressed his
satisfaction at having been chosen to preside at
the Centenary festivities to celebrate the memory
of a great apostle of Truth and Charity. The Holy
Father's words in sending him were: "Ozanam
is one of the men who have most honoured Christ
in the poor; is it not therefore right that the Pope,
Christ's representative on earth, should honour him
in his turn?"

The first meeting was held at the Catholic Institute, under the Presidency of the Right Rev. Monsignor Baudrillart, the Rector, and was attended by the members of the Council-General and a vast concourse of the brothers.

On Saturday, at the Church of the Carmelites, Mass was celebrated by Monsignor Baudrillart in the presence of the Cardinal Legate, the Cardinals of Paris, Rheims, and the Bishops attending. Holy Communion was given to 3,000 of the members present. An eloquent sermon upon the principle of Charity was preached by His Eminence Cardinal Luçon.

After the Mass, the Cardinals, accompanied by the Bishops, the members of the Council-General, and the representatives of Ozanam's family, descended to the crypt, where lie the remains of Frederic Ozanam. Prayers having been recited, the Cardinal Legate blessed the monument which has been erected to the memory of their founder by generous subscriptions from the Conferences of the Society throughout the world. The mausoleum, which rests between two pillars decorated with palms, is surmounted by a pendant in which Ozanam's profile is depicted in a medallion. The whole effect is solemn and religious, and the work is carefully carried out.

At the International General Meeting the Cardinal Legate presided, attended by the Cardinals Archbishops of Paris and Rheims; the Archbishop of

Sens; the Bishops of Amiens, Clermont, Troyes, Aire, Meaux, Moulins; Monsignor Baudrillart; the Abbé Ozanam, nephew of Frederic Ozanam; Messrs. Laporte, son-in-law and grandson of Ozanam; the Marquis de Vogué, Comte d'Haussonville, and the Presidents of many Paris charities.

After reading the customary prayers, Cardinal Vannutelli handed to the Secretary-General the following letter from the Holy Father:

TO OUR VENERABLE BROTHER VINCENT VANNU-
TELLI, CARDINAL OF THE HOLY ROMAN
CHURCH, BISHOP OF PALESTRINA.

PIUS X., POPE.

ESTEEMED BROTHER,—HEALTH AND APOSTOLIC
BENEDICTION.

We have learned that in a short time, a century having passed since the birth of Anthony Frederic Ozanam, the Society of St. Vincent de Paul is preparing to celebrate the memory of this great man by a solemn commemoration. We greatly approve of such a project, and very willingly We shall act so as to make those celebrations yet more solemn by Our participation therein. In fact, We not only find it right to honour the name of him who devoted his entire life (too short, alas!) to prove by his writings and deeds the salutary efficaciousness of the Catholic

Faith, so much so that he has been ranked among the most distinguished champions of Christian science; but neither do We wish to let the present opportunity escape, without asserting once more how much we are in favour of the work called the *Conferences*, of which Ozanam is rightly considered the principal founder. This Association, which is exclusively devoted to works of Christian Charity, and which so justly claims for itself the name and protection of St. Vincent de Paul, cannot fail to win admiration for the shortness of the time in which it has been everywhere propagated, and for the profit it has brought to all. Scarcely had Our beloved Ozanam, with a few companions actuated by the same spirit and zeal, sown its seeds, than it firmly planted its roots, and that, more promptly than people could have supposed, it grew up into a large and widespreading tree, extending its branches over the country, a development in harmony with the genius of the French nation, which no other race surpasses in activity or fecundity in undertakings calculated to promote religion. At the present time, this work of the Conferences, spread afar over the whole universe, is most useful, not only to the multitude of indigent poor, whom it provides with practical relief, both for the present life and for the world to come, but also to the members themselves, whom it trains admirably in sanctification by means of different works of Christian charity.

These considerations are quite sufficient to cause Us to be among the first to take part in the celebrations which are in preparation, and to make Us wish that the honours paid to so deserving a personage may develop among men a knowledge and a liking for his work. Assuredly, in the present great upheaval of all things, the result of false doctrines and of the licence of wicked desires, it would be extremely useful to civil society if those who are trying to give it a Christian discipline would take Ozanam for their master and guide. Accordingly, you must implore God for an ever-increasing extension of the Society of St. Vincent de Paul, in order that it may propagate in all directions, even in the most remote regions, the salutary practices for which it is indebted to its founder.

Furthermore, in the meeting which the delegates of the Conferences are about to hold in Paris, at the headquarters of the Council-General, we wish to have someone to interpret these wishes of Our inmost heart. For this purpose We see no person more fit to receive such a mission than the Cardinal of the Holy Roman Church, who has for the past twenty years been Protector of the said Society on behalf of the Apostolic See, who participates in its works, and very actively promotes its enterprises.

Accordingly, it is you, esteemed brother, whom We send as Our Legate, to express in Our name, at this assembly the sentiments We show to you by the present letter. You will also bear the Apostolic blessing, pledge of heavenly favours, to the Council-General, to the other members who, as We have just said, will be at that meeting, to all those whom the Society of St. Vincent de Paul unites together as members, or assists as poor people; to all the distinguished men, either the clergy, or the faithful, who shall have contributed in any way to enhance the said celebrations. And this blessing We give to you first of all most affectionately, esteemed brother.

Given at Rome, near St. Peter's, on the day of the Feast of Easter, in the year 1913, tenth of Our Pontificate.

Pius X., Pope.

Eloquent panegyrics upon Ozanam were then delivered by His Eminence Cardinal Vannutelli, the Cardinal-Archbishop of Paris, and by M. Calon, President-General of the Society of St. Vincent de Paul, who read out a telegram of thanksgiving which he was sending to Cardinal Merry del Val.

After a solemn blessing to the brothers of the Society by Cardinal Vannutelli, the meeting broke up. At a subsequent meeting important papers were read upon the commencement of the Society in Italy by a member of the Superior Council there, and in Belgium by the President of the Superior Council at Brussels.

The national centenary celebrations of the birth
of Frederic Ozanam, the founder of the Society of
St. Vincent de Paul, took place in Manchester on
May 30, 1913.   Although celebrations of international character were held in Paris at Easter, the
English Conferences, desirous of marking the festival
on English soil, called on the brothers to rally at
Manchester, which was considered the town most
centrally situated.   The Cardinal-Archbishop of
Westminster, the Archbishop of Liverpool, the
Bishop of Salford, other members of the Hierarchy,
and brothers from all over the country participated
in the rejoicings.   The dominant note of the three
days' proceedings was struck by the Cardinal's
thrilling appeal to the Catholic young men of
England to take up the noble work begun by
Ozanam.   The deliberations of the conferences
generally should prove of practical value.   The
Cardinal's suggestion that the brothers should
supervise the emigration of Catholic grown-up men,
and the Archbishop of Liverpool's question as to
whether the brothers could not enlarge the scope of
their activities for the poor by becoming pawnbrokers
and money-lenders, have been eagerly discussed.
Brother A. Carey, who described the attitude of the
society to the Liverpool education authority's scheme
for the after-care of school-children, contributed a
short but pregnant speech, which will doubtless
greatly influence Conferences all over the country

when they are fronted—as is likely they soon will be by the same problem.

The proceedings opened on Friday night with a large informal gathering in the Grand Hotel, to welcome the visitors. The Bishops of Salford, Sebastopolis, and Teos were present, and the former gave a short address of welcome. A programme of music was arranged for the occasion.

On Saturday morning, at eleven o'clock, a solemn High Mass of Requiem was celebrated in St. John's Cathedral, Salford, by his Lordship, Bishop Vaughan.

THE OPENING MEETING.

A great meeting was held on Saturday afternoon in St. Patrick's Hall. Long before the hour appointed, a great concourse of people lined the thoroughfares leading to St. Patrick's presbytery. The interior of the hall was gaily decorated with flags and plants, whilst a large banner in the centre had inscribed upon it " Welcome to our Cardinal."

His Eminence presided at the meeting, and was supported on the platform by the Bishop of Salford, the Bishop of Shrewsbury, Bishop Hanlon, Bishop Butt, Bishop McIntyre, Monsignor Canon O'Kelly, V.G., Very Rev. Father Joseph P. Bannin, P.S.M., Canon Sharrock, Rev. Fathers Wookey and Thomas Walsh, Alderman D. McCabe, J.P., Councillor Charles Egan, etc.

The Superior Council, in the absence of the President, Sir John Knill, Bart., was represented by Brother

F. A. R. Langton, Vice-President, Hon. A. E. Bingham, and Leonard C. Lindsay, Secretary. There were also present: Brother C. Hadfield (President of the Sheffield Council), Brother C. J. Munich, K.S.G. (London), Brother C. E. Marchall (President of the Manchester Central Council), Brother James Reynolds, P.L.G. (Treasurer of the Manchester Council), Brother James Connor (Secretary of the Manchester Council), and Brother J. Rossall.

Father Bannin opened the proceedings with prayer, after which Father Wookey gave a spiritual reading.

His Eminence the Cardinal read the following:

Telegram to the Holy Father.

"Cardinal Merry del Val, Vatican, Rome. National Ozanam Celebration in Manchester, seven Bishops present, with members of Society of St. Vincent de Paul, offers homage to His Holiness, rejoices at his recovery, begs his blessing for themselves, benefactors, and the poor" (loud applause).

The Bishop of Salford's Welcome.

The Bishop of Salford then said: "The task that has been assigned to me this afternoon is an entirely delightful one. It is one which I won't say is a duty, but is a very great privilege. It is the task of welcoming the Society of St. Vincent de Paul, not only those belonging to this county, not only those belonging to this diocese, but to the whole of England—of welcoming them to our city in order that we may celebrate the centenary of their chief founder, the great Frederic Ozanam. When I was approached some months ago with a request from the Central Council in London that the National English

Celebration of this Centenary should take place in Manchester, I need not tell you, I am sure, I felt highly flattered, and I felt, and I am sure all the Manchester brothers felt, complimented that our city should have been selected as the central point to honour the memory of Ozanam.

"I am sorry," Dr. Casartelli proceeded, "his Grace the Archbishop of Liverpool is not here this afternoon, because I should have liked to have quoted to him what one of our leading Manchester daily newspapers stated this morning in explanation of why Manchester had been chosen for this honour. It says: 'Because Manchester is the chief city of the most Catholic county in England.' I think this a most intelligent remark, and I have no doubt that this is the opinion of the Central Council of the Society of St. Vincent de Paul also, because if it is not, I cannot understand why they should have shown us this honour. In my own name, as Bishop of this diocese, in the name of my clergy, and in the name of the brothers of the local Conferences, I offer you all a most hearty and sincere welcome to this our city."

Dr. Casartelli proceeded to say that it was very gratifying to think that their visit to the city of Manchester was not unwelcome to their fellow-citizens at large. The Lord Mayor had most kindly and most cordially entered into that welcome, and had thrown open the Town Hall in honour of the brothers and their friends.

THE EARLY HISTORY OF THE SOCIETY IN ENGLAND.

A paper written by Brother Archibald J. Dunn, on "The Early History of the Society in England," was read in that gentleman's absence by Brother Lindsay.

The first beginnings of the Society in this country were due, under God, to George Jonas Wigley, a Lancashire man, who was born in Manchester in the year 1825. His father and mother having died while he was still a child, his aunt, Miss Wigley, took him to France and had him educated at the school established by Monseigneur Haffreingue in Boulogne. Later he was sent to Stonyhurst College, which he entered in the year 1837. Finishing his studies there, he returned to Paris and entered the "École des Beaux Arts" to study for his chosen profession of architect. Here he joined a group of young men, fervent Catholics, who attended the lectures at the Sorbonne of Professor Frederic Ozanam, who was at that time delivering a course on the "History of Civilization in the Fifth Century." These lectures attracted much public attention, and were furiously attacked in the anti-clerical Press. Large numbers of students from the University attended the lectures with the object of shouting down the Professor and disturbing the audience; for the followers of Rousseau and Voltaire realized that Ozanam was destroying the foundation upon which all their anti-Catholic theories had been based. In 1833 Ozanam proposed the formation of a Conference for the purpose of visiting the poor in their own homes, and seven young men at once volunteered to join him. The Archbishop of Paris warmly approved of the project, and gave it his blessing. Thus was established the first Conference of the S. V. P. The rules had been drawn up with French precision, and Wigley translated them into English. He sent them to his friend, Frederick Lucas, and urged upon him to establish a Conference of the Society in London. Wigley, as soon as he had taken his diploma as an architect, returned to London to practise his profession. Eventually, having already watched the progress of the Society in France, Wigley called upon Bishop Griffiths, in London, the Vicar-Apostolic of the London district at the time, and sought his interest. The Bishop warmly approved of the proposal, and invited several prominent and influential Catholics to meet and establish the Society. Wigley acted as provisional secretary. Mr. Fred Lucas was elected the first president, but on his refusal, Mr. Pagliano was offered and accepted the post. This was in the year 1844. The London conference was affiliated to that in Paris, and the rules of the English Society were printed, and the work commenced at Mr. Pagliano's Hotel, the Sablonière, in Leicester Square. In 1848 Wigley repaired to Paris to help Brother Ozanam in the trying times of the Revolution, and they were both witnesses to the death of the saintly Archbishop of Paris, who was shot down in the streets. When the Revolution was ended Wigley went to Rome, and was created by Pius IX. a Knight of St. Sylvester, as a reward for his services to the Church. Returning later to England, Brother Wigley entered actively into the work of the Society, joining the Conference of Warwick Street, London. " I first met Brother Wigley," writes the author of this paper, " at meetings of the London Council in 1857. The president then was Brother George Blount, and the other members were Brothers Renfric and Henry Arundell, J. Sidney Lescher, Charles Corney, John Stuart Knill, John St. Lawrence, S. J. Nicholl, J. J. H. Saint, Hubert Jerningham, and George Wigley, who was foreign secretary." The paper

6

next reviewed Wigley's incursions into Catholic journalism, at the request of Cardinal Wiseman, and also his great work (again with the Society at his back) as secretary of the St. Peter's Pence Association—an organization which assisted the Pope financially in the period following the Italian Revolution. This Society, which owed its inception to Wigley, was a success, as much as £300 per month being sent to Rome. Poor Wigley eventually died of fever in Italy, contracted through attending a fever-stricken sailor. He was an Oriental scholar, and had the reputation of understanding seventeen languages, always a most amiable and kind-hearted man, but very unconventional. He was very proud of being a " Lancashire lad," and prophesied that the Society of St. Vincent de Paul would flourish more in the North than in the South of England.

In the discussion which followed, Father Wookey asked whether the prophecy of Brother Wigley had as yet been fulfilled. If the reply was in the negative, was it not time they made a start to see to its fulfilment?

Father Bannin, who has charge of the Italian parish in London, disputed the claim that the initiative of the St. Vincent de Paul Society in this country was altogether due to Brother Wigley. On behalf of the Italians, the Reverend speaker claimed that Ozanam was born in Milan, and was, therefore, an Italian. Brother Wigley was a cosmopolitan. His family now resided in Milan; he died in Rome; and he was a man who spoke almost every language upon the earth except his own mother tongue. In fact, he was half Manchester and half Italian. Father Bannin also maintained that Brother Pagliano, an Italian, was the first president of any English Conference.

Father Bannin concluded by saying that the Society might yet hope to see Frederic Ozanam, although a layman, upon the altars of the Church. There was no reason why the cause of his Beatification should not go on. He asked them all to pray unceasingly that Frederic Ozanam might soon be found worthy of that great honour and dignity (applause).

Brother C. E. Marshall (president of the Manchester Council), in the course of an address, said he had suggested to the Superior Council that the Society should take charge in some way or other of the Catholic emigrants leaving this country. They knew that there were a great number year by year who left these shores for the Colonies, and they heard from brothers in various parts that Catholics, or at least many of them, who emigrated, were led astray, either on the voyage or just after landing. Mr. Marshall submitted that the local branches should ascertain all possible particulars about intending emigrants, and keep the London Council fully posted up. The Superior Council would then know what Catholic emigrants would be on board a particular steamer, and a chaplain and other Catholics travelling on the same steamer might be asked to interest themselves in the emigrants. By these means Catholics would get to know one another on the voyage, and therein safeguards to many would be assured. The names of the emigrants and all particulars could be sent to the various ports in the Colonies, where the brothers would meet the steamers.

His Eminence Cardinal Bourne stated that at the present time the North had as many as 2,812 members, and the South 3,011. When they came to analyze them, however, they would find that in the North there were

2,089 active members, and in the South 1,731. In the North again, there were 725 honorary members and in the South 1,276. So they would see that there was plenty of room for development both in the North and South. In congratulating Mr. Archibald Dunn on his interesting paper concerning the early days of the Society in England, the Cardinal said that names were mentioned in that account, the memories of which ought certainly never ·to be lost in this country. Men such as Bishop Griffiths, who welcomed the Society, and Frederick Lucas, who did untold good for the Church in this country, vigorously—sometimes, perhaps, too vigorously—but who certainly did an immense work for the Church of God as editor of the *Tablet*. And the next was Brother Wigley, whose name was almost forgotten. The account given to them, proceeded his Eminence, was of special interest to himself. It brought back the fact to their minds that in the early days·their Society in England was known as the Brotherhood of St. Vincent de Paul. One of the early Conferences was founded at St. Edmund's College, Old Hall, Ware, and that Conference survived to this day. He himself was a member of it, and it had always been known in that College as the Brotherhood of St. Vincent de Paul. And in alluding to that fact he would like to express the hope and the wish that, whatever the name of the Society might be, it might always be permeated by that spirit of brotherhood which it had had from the beginning.

No suggestion, continued the Cardinal, that had been made at any recent meeting of the Society of St. Vincent de Paul appeared to him more worthy of attention than that regarding emigration. This question of the care of their emigrants was a very pressing one indeed. All their various Rescue Societies had been coalesced into a Catholic Emigration Society, and considerable provision had thus been made for the emigration of boys and girls to Canada, but no such provision had, as far as he knew, been made in connection with other parts of the British Empire. Until a short time ago no provision even for women emigrating to Canada existed, but now, thanks to the efforts of the Catholic Women's League, due provision had been made. A hostel had been started in Liverpool by them, and Catholic women, who intended going to Canada, would have the opportunity, if they cared to avail themselves of it, of emigrating under Catholic auspices. But, so far as he knew, there were no provisions whatever for Catholic grown-up men going out anywhere under the auspices of any Catholic Society; they had no provision for the emigration of Catholics, whether men or women, boys or girls, to any other part of the world. He had been speaking lately to the recently appointed Bishop of Calgary, and the feeling was expressed that the great thing was, if possible, to get Catholics to emigrate to some centre where Catholics already resided in numbers, or failing that to get their people to emigrate in groups and form a settlement in the new Canadian countries. If Catholics in twos and threes settled in places where Catholics were not numerous, they were in great danger of being very easily absorbed into non-Catholic communities around them. In many places there was no Catholic church at all, whilst the nearest priest obtainable was some fifty miles away. The churches in these rising townships in Western Canada were, as everywhere else, the centres of social intercourse on Sundays. People came in from farms situated sometimes at great distances, and, for the sake of social intimacy, drifted towards the Episcopalian, the Presbyterian, or the Wesleyan chapels. If Catholic emigrants could be persuaded by Catholic Societies to go either to those places where Catholics already existed in numbers, or arrange to emigrate in groups and start a Catholic centre, not only would they be protected to a large extent against the loss of their own faith, but they would be the means of building up the Catholic Church in Canada. All the Bishops in the Western parts of Canada were of the same opinion. They had no Society whatever to look after the men of their Faith who emigrated, so if the Society of St. Vincent de Paul would take in hand this duty, with that devotedness, earnestness, and world-wide charity known to them, he did not know of any greater work of charity that could be committed to their care.

His Eminence spoke also of the emigration to New Zealand and Australia. In the former country Catholics had representation on a committee that was formed for dealing with emigrants, but they had no Catholic Society to deal with boys and young men who wished to go to Australia. The field out there for emigrants was simply enormous, and the area was almost inconceivable. He was speaking the other day to the Catholic Bishop of Perth, Western Australia, who told him that, when he wished to visit certain parts of his vast diocese, he had to undertake a journey necessitating a sea passage of four whole days. The day must come, sooner or later, his Eminence concluded, when they would find that Catholics would be setting their faces in the direction of emigration to Australia, and it was, therefore, very important indeed that some organization should be set on foot to deal with it, and with all his heart he welcomed the suggestion of Brother Marshall, and trusted that the Society of St. Vincent de Paul would be able to put it into practice as soon as possible.

MAYORAL RECEPTION.

The Right Hon. the Lord Mayor of Manchester (Mr. H. W. Royse) had intended to hold a reception at the Town Hall on Saturday evening, to welcome His Eminence the Cardinal, the Bishops, and the visiting brothers of the Society. As many as 1,200 invitations were sent out. His Lordship, owing to an unfortunate indisposition, was prevented at the last moment from attending the function, and his place was taken by the Lady Mayoress and Dr. Fraser and Mrs. Fraser. The reception—unique so far as Manchester is concerned—was a brilliant affair.

THE PARAMOUNT NEED.

YOUNG MEN AND THE SOCIETY'S WORK.

Cardinal Bourne presided over the mass meeting of the delegates and the general body of Manchester Catholics, held in the Free Trade Hall, on Sunday afternoon. His Eminence was accompanied on the platform by the Archbishop of Liverpool, the Bishop of Salford, Bishops McIntyre, Hanlon, and Vaughan, Mgr. Canon O'Kelly, V.G., Mgr. Jackman, D.D., the Mayor of Battersea (Brother T. Brogan), and a representative body of clergy and laity.

The Mayor of Battersea, who delivered an eloquent address, said that the brothers were fighting together for the great common cause for the common good of the common people. Europe was an armed camp. The Cross and the Crescent had again been in conflict, and thousands of the dead were lying unburied on the battle-fields of the Near East. In the factory, in the work-shop, in the office, the brothers of St. Vincent de Paul had to preach the great lesson of Christian charity their great Founder had implanted in their hearts. They had to spread the noble gospel that the great work of life was not to destroy life, but to preserve it. They had to show to the world that the spirit of Frederic Ozanam was alive in their hearts to-day, and that it was growing up a great, powerful, dominant force, which would eventually make England a better England, the Empire a better Empire, and the world a better world. But there was other work than this—work nearer to hand and, perhaps, more easy of immediate accomplishment. In the richest country of the world, with the wealth of the world pouring into her coffers—in a land as beautiful as a poet's dream, with a soil as fruitful as God's own love, with a climate as sweet as a mother's smile, and teeming with inexhaustible mineral wealth, there were thousands perishing of hunger and starvation. Proceed-ing, his Worship alluded to the Mayoral reception of the previous evening in the greatest industrial beehive in all the world. That was a proof, he declared, that Catholicity was at last coming into her own again in England. People were finding out that Catholics, after all, did a little bit for the poor, although they did not proclaim it from the housetops. There were people who did not know of the tremendous amount of money

Catholics saved the State every year in the poor-rate by looking after their own poor. There were those who did not realize—until it càme to an education fight—that Catholics saved the State millions every year by educating their own children. The Catholic Church was the greatest factor in the world for the training and building up of moral character, the greatest factor in the world for looking after the poor, and the greatest factor in the world for the education of children.

Cardinal Bourne said that Bishop McIntyre's eloquent sermon and the Mayor of Battersea's address had suggested two thoughts to his mind. The first was that, when the founders of the St. Vincent de Paul Society began their work sixty years ago, they certainly never foresaw the developments the work would attain. As far as France was concerned, the present generation had great reason to be thankful to Almighty God that what Ozanam wrote seventy years ago would not be true to-day. There had been progress, and there had been progress all along the line, and it was only by looking back over a long period of years that they could realize that those forces of evil which were so powerful seventy years ago had certainly been weakened very considerably in the time that had elapsed. And he thought that, whilst they must not shut their eyes to the evils that surrounded them, it would be unworthy of them, and derogatory also to the honour and glory of God, were they not fully to recognize the things that had been accomplished by Divine grace. Here in England in those sixty years, his Eminence proceeded, the Catholic Church had certainly gained a power and position and influence—an influence for the exercise of charity that was not given to her hitherto. The second thought was this, the Cardinal went on: Had the Society of St. Vincent de Paul here in England made the progress it ought to have made in the last sixty years? Sixty years ago, or a little over sixty years ago, at the time of the introduction of the Society into this country, the ecclesiastical hierarchy of England had not been restored, and progress was hindered in many directions. But since then Catholics had seen a remarkable growth in the number of their Bishops and clergy, in the number of religious houses, charitable institutions, churches, schools, and the children attending those schools. That progress had been very great indeed. He did not say it had been more than they might have hoped for, but it had been more than was hoped for sixty years ago. While it had certainly been great, it might have been greater. How had things gone with the Society of St. Vincent de Paul? When they recognized that there were in this country something between 5,000 or 6,000 members of the Society, he was sure they must recognize also that despite its magnificent aims the progress had not been what it ought to have been. He did not like to sound a note of sadness or a note of criticism in the midst of the celebrations, but if they wanted to do better in the future it was only right to see whether or not they had done as well as they might have done in the past. " Your work," his Eminence pointed out, " is a work for laymen, and especially for young laymen. I say that with special emphasis to-day, because, to our very great regret, it is brought home to us that some of the older members who have stood in the forefront and been your leaders in the past are absent from these celebrations by reason of years and failing health, and their absence is a call for the young men to step into the ranks and take their places. Men like Brother Count Torre Diaz, Brother Hemelryk, and Brother President Sir John Knill —although Sir John is a younger man—gladly though they would have come, are not here to-day, simply and solely because ill-health prevented them. Their absence brings home with special force the fact that with the older workers falling out and passing to their reward, it is to the young men we must look to carry on the work of the Society."

What was the inspiring motive that, amongst other things, led Frederic Ozanam to begin his work? He saw young men round about him on whatever side attacked, as all young men are to some extent, and always will be, and are especially at the present day— attacked by those incitements to scepticism and to loss of virtue which are always amongst the most potent causes of the leakages we so constantly deplore. We must not shut our eyes to these facts. At the present day, when young men enter on life, equipped perhaps only with such religious instruction as they have been able to obtain in our elementary schools, they are met in the office and workshop by other young men who, in a few specious words, are able to put before them objections which seem to strike at the very root of Catholic Faith. It is always easy to make objections; it is always easy for the flippant and the superficial to catch up an objection out of some sixpenny handbook, and then hurl it at the head of the Catholic young man, who not infrequently, having present to his mind no complete and adequate answer, is sometimes apt to forget that when he is dealing with the things of Almighty God, he is often dealing with matters of mystery, which, taken by themselves, have to be looked at with the eye of faith, although, regarded in their connection with the Christian revelation; the eye of reason can find no flaw in them. If such a young man is not careful, and does not watch over himself, he may be brought to the threshold of the loss of his soul. We know that this is going on: Ozanam in his day knew it was going on. What did he do? He said to these young men: "Get to know the real conditions of life. Go amongst the poor. See their lives, understand their difficulties; and then ask yourselves whether it is not the revelation of Jesus Christ alone that can answer the questions of those sorely stricken hearts?" He put them in the way of overcoming the difficulties urged upon them, not by direct answer, but by showing them that the problems of life, which many men, and especially young men, feel so acutely, cannot be solved by the specious theories of the objector but can be solved only by the Gospel which God has given to us. Then we know how many are led astray by the uprising vices which attack them in early manhood. They pass from the practice of their religion because their hearts are in a turmoil of confusion by the unruled and unruly affections that afflict them. To such young men in his day Frederic Ozanam said: "Go down amongst the poor and see their sufferings, and help them. In that self-sacrifice you will find the very elements that will enable you to govern your own poor faltering hearts." From that point of view alone, his Eminence went on to declare, the Society of St. Vincent de Paul was a necessity to the Catholic young men of to-day. If a young man wished to keep bright and clear his Faith, if he wished to preserve unsullied and unspotted his virtue, there was no surer way than by becoming a devoted and earnest member of the Society of St. Vincent de Paul. Did they ask how they might better understand what should be the work of the Society in England, he would answer that the only way was to go back to those principles úpon which the Society was built up.

CALL FOR PERSONAL SERVICE.

They must begin by remembering that the Society was not a mere relieving society. What their founder called upon them to do was to give personal service to the poor in every way they could. Very often the best and most potent service they could render was what any man with a heart could give, even if he had not a penny in his pocket. Men and women there were to-day amongst the poor who were crushed to the very heart, and could not look up to Heaven because they were so heavily laden, and the man who went amongst them, and could say a kind word, would lift up their hearts to higher things and make them look with confidence for a better day—such a one was a true brother of St. Vincent de Paul, even though he never gave a sixpence. The young men round Frederic Ozanam had, no doubt, very little indeed to give. They were students of law, doctors just beginning to practise, men in different walks of life, and what Ozanam asked of them was to give freely of personal service, each using the individual talents of his profession. In every position of life to-day there were men who were able to give of their fuller knowledge of some particular department of life, which would be of help and guidance to the poor they visited. He feared that a good many young men were held back from joining the Society because they had nothing to give. Let them understand that it was not money, but personal service that was required. The Cardinal next suggested that if the Society

was to increase and spread it must be governed by loyalty
to the traditions of its founder and a spirit of progress
that moved along traditional lines.   Many things existed
to-day which did not exist in the days of Frederic Ozanam:
many problems were before them which Ozanam could
not foresee.   But the Society must not set those things
aside as unworthy of their attention ; they must not with-
draw from the consideration of those problems simply
because Ozanam did not know them.   Let them be filled
with his spirit, and when in their work there arose something needing to be done, which no one was doing and
no one was prepared to do; when some problem faced
them which needed tackling, and was not being tackled—
let them ask themselves whether it might not be that the
very spirit, the very vitality, and the very principles of
Frederic Ozanam urged them to take that work in hand.
An instance of a work that required attending to, and to
which no one, so far as he knew, had as yet attempted to
attend, was that of superintending the emigration of
Catholic grown-up men.   The organization of the Society
of St. Vincent de Paul was represented all over the world,
and probably no other organization could take the work
in hand with such prospect of success.

Catholic Women's League and the Catenian Association.

   " He trusted that it would not be taken amiss if he
alluded to the work of the Catholic Women's League.
One of the secrets of the success of the Women's League
was that its members had so readily accepted local conditions, and tried to do work that had to be done, and that
no one else would do.   He had also heard recently, and
with very great satisfaction, of the formation of a new

Catholic Society, which he believed had taken its birth in Manchester. He referred to the Catenian Association. This association banded together a large number of Catholic business and professional men in all parts of the country, and he hoped that it would be very useful to its members in their worldly concerns and the advancement of their children. But he would ask the members of the association with all earnestness to devote their energy and some part of their leisure time to the work of the St. Vincent de Paul Society. And if God had blessed them with sons, he would remind them that there was no greater advantage they could bestow upon their sons in their early manhood than that of letting them join the Society of St. Vincent de Paul."

The Archbishop of Liverpool said that he had more poor in his diocese than had any of the Bishops present. The poor, his Grace went on, as the Brothers well knew, appreciated sympathy far more than material assistance. Proceeding, his Grace raised the question of patronage work, which, he said, was rather differently conducted in different parts of the country. Through the co-operation of the Bishop of Salford, the Brothers of the whole of Lancashire had an annual meeting to discuss that and other phases of their work, with the greatest benefit. He recommended the practice as one that might be taken up with advantage all over the country.

Continuing, his Grace remarked that the poor had two great friends. One was the pawnshop, and the other, also a deadly enemy, was the money-lender. He had often wondered when he thought of the *mont de piété* of the Catholic countries on the Continent, whether it would not be possible for the Brothers of St. Vincent de Paul to take up a somewhat similar work. In other words, could the Brothers run a pawnshop? Money-lending was another subject he thought they might tackle. The clergy and people had made a start in Liverpool in one of the poorest Catholic parishes, and the movement, though at present only on a small scale, inspired the hope that it was going to be a success. The great port of Liverpool, with its sea-going population, was obsessed by the demon of casual labour, and, as a result, by the curse of money-lending. The wives of the seamen, through no fault of their own, could not make ends meet, owing to the long intervals between their husbands' pay-days. If the Brothers of St. Vincent de Paul could devise some means of helping these poor and deserving women, incalculable benefits would be the result. Could the Brothers become money-lenders—beneficent money-lenders?

The After-Care of Children.

Brother Carey, who represented Brother Hemelryk, K.C.S.G., O.R.S., President of the Liverpool Central Council, alluded to the scheme for the after-care of children which has been devised by the Liverpool Education Authority. The authorities, the speaker pointed out, wished to entrust the scheme, so far as was possible, to voluntary workers. Considering the interests involved, and the influence that such voluntary workers would naturally gain in the households they visited, it was extremely desirable—more than that, absolutely necessary —that none but a Catholic should visit a Catholic family. The scheme, which, he believed, would later on be adopted all over the country, had been carefully discussed by the Brothers in Liverpool a few days ago, as they were convinced that it was a case in which their activities would be of very special value. It had been decided that they should accept the principle of the scheme, but only subject to certain conditions and with certain reservations as to detail. One of those reservations was that under no circumstances should the Brothers undertake duties which would cause the poor to look on them as officials. Another was that they should not be required to divulge information which had been given to them in confidence.

The Bishop of Salford, in moving a vote of thanks to the Cardinal, the Archbishop, the Bishops, the Mayor of Battersea, and Brother Carey, said that never before in the history of Manchester had a Catholic gathering received such honour at the hands of the municipal authorities. He could not sufficiently express the gratitude and admiration felt by Catholics for the gracious and charming manner in which the Lady Mayoress had welcomed the delegates at the civic reception the previous evening. His lordship also expressed the hope that there would be a great influx of new blood into the Society. Zealous recruiting work, he was convinced, would result in the Society having a membership not of 6,000, but of 60,000 at the end of twelve months.

THE BANQUET.

On Sunday evening, 750 guests sat down to dinner in the Midland Hotel. The President of the Manchester Particular Council (Mr. C. E. Marshall) presided, having on his right his Eminence Cardinal Bourne and on his left his Grace the Archbishop of Liverpool. There were also present the Bishop of Salford, Bishop Vaughan, Bishop McIntyre, Bishop Butt, Bishop Hanlon, Monsignor O'Kelly, V.G., Monsignor Poock, D.D., Canon Sharrock, Monsignor Jackman, D.D., Father Bader, S.J., Rev.

Dr. Hohn, Rev. F. Gonne, M.A., Rev. J. McNulty M.A., etc.

During the evening Cardinal Bourne read a telegram from the Holy Father conveying his blessing to all who had taken part in the celebration.

THE EVILS OF SOCIETY AND OZANAM'S REMEDY.*

FUTILITY OF NON-CHRISTIAN EFFORT.

" By charity of the Spirit serve one another."—GAL. v. 13.

IF Frederic Ozanam's life is judged only by its duration, it will' seem an unfinished and broken life, for he died a comparatively young man ; but if it is judged by its intensity, it will be found a full and well-rounded life. He began to put forth his intellectual strength even in early youth, and that strength was recognized by the most brilliant and noted men of France, some of whom have left their testimony to the precocity of his genius, the power of his understanding, and his admirable moral qualities.　Much has been written of him, because there was much to tell of his extraordinary talents, and of his activities as student, as historian, as man of letters, as social reformer, and as Christian apologist.　Interest, too, would be found in the accounts left to us of his beautifully winning character—his urbanity and pleasantness, his gentleness and courtesy.　A contemporary said of him : " He takes away your heart and gives you his own."　It

* A sermon to the delegates of the St. Vincent de Paul Society, preached at St. John's Cathedral, Salford, by his Lordship, the Bishop of Lamus (the Right Rev. John McIntyre, D.D.).

would be interesting to speak of these things, but at present we are more concerned in those things which have won for him a world-wide reverence—his warm charity, his unfailing tenderness for the afflicted and his devotedness of service to them, all of which have found permanent expression in the Society of St. Vincent de Paul. Therefore, laying all else aside, I propose to speak only of what has reference to your Society. I will try, first of all, to set before you the circumstances out of which the thought came to him which afterwards grew into the Society of St. Vincent, and, next, I will try to describe the broad and lofty motives which inspired his labours in building up the Society. From that description you will see that there was a moral unity binding together all the activities of Ozanam's life. They sprang from one chief motive, and were directed to one chief end. I trust that even my imperfect account of these things may be received by you with such good-will that every brother will return from this celebration resolved to love the Society more, and to labour more for its advance.

The main portion of Ozanam's life fell in troubled and dangerous times. He was seventeen years of age when the Revolution of 1830, overturning the throne of Charles X., began to gather further strength for the greater Revolution of 1848. The King in his fall seemed to pull down with him the power and influence of the Church of France. The forces of private thought, as well as those of public life, began to be directed in bitterness against her. So completely did men become estranged from Religion, so utterly did they neglect its practice, that the sight of a man in church caused as great a sensation as the sight of a Christian traveller in an Oriental mosque. Priests were afraid to go in their ordinary dress along the public streets. What was proudly called intellectual enlightenment was regarded as having obtained so complete a triumph over the Faith that the very suggestion of the possibility of a revival was received with a general outburst of amused or contemptuous laughter. It was quite taken for granted that the Faith was dead, that now, at last, it really was dead and buried, and nothing further was required but that the philosophers, men of letters, and politicians should seal the stone of its sepulchre. Ozanam could not but feel the influences of the time, for who could altogether escape them? Who was safe when a wild flood of thought was carrying away a whole population? In early youth Ozanam found that the waves of doubt were rising about him and beginning to roll over his head; and although he was too strong to be pulled under, they nevertheless filled him with terror and caused him a struggle of bitter agony. His faith triumphed over every doubt, and the trial through which he had passed was providentially turned to good account. In the providence of God that assault on Ozanam's faith became the occasion of the Society of St. Vincent de Paul. Ozanam had not only gained a deep insight into the nature of the intellectual malady that was infecting the mind of his countrymen, but he had also learned compassion for those who had been less fortunate than himself in escape from that malady. He wished to come to their assistance, and it was this " charity of the spirit " that prompted his first social efforts. This was a true charity of the spirit, for the spirit which is of God is a spirit of truth and faith as well as of consolation. Ozanam's first apostolate was an apostolate of the mind. For the sake of this apostolate he determined to become a professor and writer; and to fit himself for the work he studied as much as sixteen and even eighteen hours a day. It is well to remember that his first conferences were started as a ministry of intellectual charity. His desire was to band studious young men together under the standard of Catholic thought; for, to use his own words, " our Faith always remains young, and as fully equipped for meeting the needs of every age as for healing the wounds of every soul." But by the side of this first compassion there grew up another compassion in his heart; it was for the toiling masses, who were suffering loss of other things besides loss of Faith. A double misery was upon them; for not only were they exploited by employers, who forced from them the largest possible amount of labour for the smallest possible wage, but, moreover, while being thus robbed in this world, they were being deluded into giving up their hope of the next world. The thought of this double misery weighed upon Ozanam's soul, and he formed a plan of getting others to join him in a noble crusade against the ignorance, the want, and the misery of the masses. The purposes that were running through his head were set forth in a kind of manifesto: " We are like the Samaritan of the Gospel," he wrote. " We have seen society prostrate and astray from her true road, robbed and beaten as she has been by robbers of the understanding. And the priest and the Levite who were passing did not pass by; they drew near in kindness, but she, in her delirium, was afraid of them and resented their approach. We, therefore, whom she does not know, desire to come to her aid and to pour oil into her wounds. We would raise her from the dust, and place her, soothed and calmed, in the hands of the Church—of that Divine hostess who will give her food and guidance to complete her pilgrim journey to immortality." You will observe, first, that telling phrase—"robbers of the understanding." The mind of the people was being plundered of the treasure of truth. You will observe, next, that Ozanam's remedy for the evils of society was, that society should be brought back and placed under the care and guidance of the Church. Further, that it should be brought back by laymen, for it had become afraid of the priest. In no other way could he see perfect deliverance. Now, the striking thing about this suggestion is that at that time Ozanam had not studied the history of the Church as he came to study it later, and was not in a position properly to appreciate the marvellous resources of the Church's healing power. The fuller and clearer knowledge came later. Writing eight years later, in 1843, he said : " I have experienced how much we gain from a close study of Christianity. Certainly I was not ignorant of its benefits, but I have discovered that they have been far greater than I had ever imagined. More than ever do I feel how much we ought to love the Church, which has done so much to preserve us, to train us, and to make possible whatever we possess of learning, of intelligence, of liberty, and of civilization." But although Ozanam had not yet learned all that he afterwards learned about the healing power of the Church, he already knew enough to perceive that the spirit and teaching of the Church would be more beneficial to society than the spirit and teaching of unbelieving social reformers; that the teaching of the Church not only contained all that there was of truth and value in the current schemes of social reform, but also preserved that truth free from the dangers and illusions of self-interest; and that even if the schemes of the social reformers were free from danger, they were still insufficient of themselves and stood in need of Catholic principle to bring about the triumph of peace as well as of justice. When Ozanam's mind had grown mature in the study of the social question, he expressed his deep fears as to the dangers in the economic theories that were being proposed as a solution. They seemed to him to lead to a conflict of selfishness. It would become a system of strike and striking back. On the one side, there was the theory of free competition, and this tempted the employer to grow rich from the competition for employment among the workers; on the other side, there was the theory of a more equitable distribution, and he feared that in urging this the organizers of labour were in danger of exciting in the workers the same spirit of greed for which they condemned the employers. This would be selfishness against selfishness; and men needed the Apostle's warning: "If you bite and devour one another, take heed that you be not consumed of one another." Which ever side won, he thought that the victory could only bring a truce; it would not bring permanent peace. To secure perfect peace, he believed that men must learn from the Church not only a sincere love of justice, but also a love of that true and real brotherhood which they can find only in Christ. Peace and justice would reign when men had learned to respect in each other the image of God, and when they cherished that fellowship to which they are called in the Incarnate Son of God, the Redeemer of all. These are the judgments of his later years; but with a power of insight marvellous in a young man of twenty-three, he had written as early as the year 1836: "The question which now divides men is no longer a political question; it is a social question. The question is this: Which will prevail—the spirit of egoism or the spirit of sacrifice? will society be exploited by the strong, or will it become the consecration of each for the good of all, and especially for the protection of the weak? There are many who have too much, and who wish to have still more: there are many more who have not enough, who have nothing, and who wish to take if it is not given to them. Between these two classes a conflict is preparing, and it threatens to be a terrible one, for on the one side there will be the power of gold, and on the other the power of despair." These words ring in our ears with all the clearness of actuality; but it is well to remember that the forecast was made by Ozanam seventy-seven years ago. He foresaw the danger, and he called upon Catholic young men to come with their Catholic principles to interpose between the two armies, and, if they could not prevent the conflict, at least try to lessen the shock. But even if economic systems were far more effective for good, than hitherto they have proved to be, there would still remain open a wide field for the exercise of that "charity of the spirit" of which the Apostle speaks: "By charity of the spirit serve one another." For after all is said and done, man is much more than a body with needs and appetites, and his inward peace comes from something higher than the mere contentment of bodily needs and appetites. There are heartaches and miseries of the soul, and sorrow may take hold of the spirit in the midst of material abundance. It was in the design of the Society of St. Vincent to pour the oil and balm of charity into the wounds of the soul also. This is a form of help which brings no hints of inferiority in the recipient, and cannot create any sense of shame in those who stand in need of it; rather, it elevates both giver and receiver, for it is a sign of their sacred union in that Divine charity which is the bond of perfection.

Meantime there is great need of the other forms of charity also. Politicians and economists have not yet succeeded in banishing from our midst bodily miseries and wretchedness, and the charitable work of alleviating them must still go on. In fact, the need of ministering to the afflicted in body has been so urgent that it holds a prominent place in the actual work of your Society. This was Ozanam's final step in his vindication of the Church. When he spoke to the men of Paris in praise of the Church and in commendation of her power to heal the evils of society, it was said to him: " If you speak of the past, what you say is true. Christianity did do wonders, but now it is played out. What works are you doing to prove your faith and to make us respect and believe it ?" Ozanam felt the full force of the retort and resolved to remove further occasion for it. He said to his Catholic friends: " We must bestir ourselves, and make our action agree with our faith. Let us, therefore, turn to the assistance of the needy, and so put our faith under the protection of charity." In this you have the true motto of the Society—Faith under the protection of charity. The Society was created to be a vindication of the Church by the exercise of charity in the widest meaning of the word—charity for mind, charity for heart, charity for body, charity for the whole man— full and perfect service to our neighbour by charity of the spirit. The Society was intended to be a proof of the healing power of Christianity, a testimony before men of the truth and beneficence of the Church. Is

that idea too ambitious ?   Ozanam would have replied
that no one can measure the power of charity ; that he
had no intention of grappling with the whole world, but
that he could begin with a few of the poor and allow the
work to grow by its own vitality, and to spread silently
over the earth.   And most wonderfully has it spread.
Ozanam himself was indefatigable in labouring for
it.   Wherever he went, whether for study, or for holiday,
or in search of health, he at once established a Conference.   This he did in Spain, France, Italy, Germany,
and even here in England.   I have read that to-day
the Society counts 7,000 Conferences with more than
140,000 brothers.   A Society which has already grown
so strong gives reasonable hope of becoming a mighty
power for good in the Church and in the world.

But the members must remain true to the noble
and generous spirit of Ozanam, and hold fast to the
faith that was in him, and which he commended to
the brethren in his last will and testament: " I die
in the bosom of the Church Catholic, Apostolic, and
Roman.   I have known the doubts of the age, but the
whole of my life has convinced me that there is no
rest for the mind and heart except in the Church and
under her authority.   If I attach any value to my
prolonged studies it is because they give me the right
to beseech all those whom I love that they remain
faithful to a religion in which I found light and
peace."

O lofty-souled, noble-hearted young man, knowing
you as we do, we are not surprised to hear the Vicar
of Christ say : " I have no stronger wish than that the
life and spirit of Frederic Ozanam should spread to
the ends of the earth."   And you, brothers, here

assembled, do you take those words of the Sovereign Pontiff not only as a wish, but also as a promise and a prophecy.

OZANAM AS A DEMOCRAT.

By Rev. H. Day, S.J.*

WE are celebrating the occurrence of a centenary, he said, which reflects a world glory on the beliefs and practice, the faith and charity of the Catholic Church. The central figure of the picture it represents is a young man of the middle class, of Jewish descent, of delicate health, but, withal, of high intellectual capacity, and of supreme moral courage. His name is Frederic Ozanam : his calling that of a Professor of Literature at the famous University of the Sorbonne in Paris. The background of the picture is gloomy enough : Paris after the great Revolution, honeycombed with infidelity and seething with scepticism, and still filled with the rancour of Voltaire's bitter wit and hatred of Christianity. The churches were everywhere empty and deserted. The French Hierarchy were afraid and silent. The schools were frankly unbelieving. Ozanam looked out upon his country and saw its faith and freedom in a pitiful plight. He resolved to rescue it from both these dangers, and set himself to the work in the spirit of a splendid hope. " I felt," he says of himself, " that the past was falling to pieces, that the foundation of the building we have known are shaken, that an earthquake has changed the whole face of the earth. But I believed in Providence, and I did not despair of my country." Amidst the wreck

* Delivered in the Church of the Holy Name, Manchester.

of social and political institutions, he took his stand on
the bed-rock of human life—the essential truth of religion,
the revelation of God, His Providence proclaiming itself
throughout the ages in history, His inscrutable wisdom
guiding man's destiny, His immutable power sustaining
and shaping the changing world. That foundation for
him was the Catholic Faith unfolding itself in Catholic
Charity. " These are the things," he said, " which
society needs, and these are the things which I equally
need."

His faith was a Virile Intellectual Faith—a faith
which, like steel, had been tempered in the fire of
temptation, and strengthened by prayer and study.
Referring to the past and to his student days, he said :
" God gave me the grace to be born in the Faith.
Later, the confusion of an unbelieving world surrounded
me. I knew all the horrors of the doubts that torment
the soul. It was then that the instructions of a priest
and philosopher saved me. I believed thenceforth with
an assured faith, and touched by so rare a goodness, I
promised God to devote my life to the service of the
Truth which had given me peace." Rarely was a promise
more faithfully kept. In his lectures and in his writings
he brilliantly defended Catholic Faith against all comers.
And the atmosphere of the faith permeated every one of
his numerous scientific and literary works. " Those who
desire to see no religion introduced into science," he
wrote, " accuse me of a lack of independence. But I
pride myself on such an accusation. I do not aspire to
an independence, the result of which is to believe and to
love nothing." Conscious that his soul was made for
God, he lived and worked so as to make himself worthy
of this lofty calling. Prayer and the Sacraments were

his constant recourse; and his charity towards God and his neighbour were commensurate with his faith. So that when, at the close of his life, at the age of forty, the priest exhorted him to have confidence in God, swift came the reply from his lips: "Oh, why should I fear God, whom I love so much?" Such was Ozanam the Catholic. He stood out in a pagan and unregenerate age a man apart, a man alive with faith and supernatural love. There is another phase of his life to consider hardly less interesting or useful. Frederic Ozanam was a Catholic and a democrat. He believed that a Christian Democracy was the end towards which Providence was leading the world; and he saw in the Christian revelation and in the traditional teaching of the Church the germs of an ideal of government, which he expressed in the formula: "The self-sacrifice of each for the benefit of all." "This," he added, "was the Christian Republic of the Primitive Church of Jerusalem; and it will probably be the form of government in the time to come." His dream was to unite the master forces of Catholicism and Freedom—a dream which has since, to some extent, been realized, and is still being increasingly fulfilled. The masses of the people, not the classes, were, in his conviction, the opportunity and the hope of the Church. "I have always believed," he wrote, when things were at their worst, "in the possibility of Christian Democracy: indeed, as far as politics go, I believe in nothing else." Like Lacordaire, he was "a Liberal to the last." Above all, he insisted that it was the social question and not any political issue which was essential. At the same time, he was fully alive to the eventualities of politics, and he was not afraid of the impending changes which he believed to be inevitable, and a part of the Divine dispensation for the development of society on the lines of a higher freedom and purer morality. When France was again on the verge of revolution in 1848, addressing the members of the Catholic Club, he urged them boldly to cast aside the dynastic politicians and to take their stand openly with the people. The outcome of Ozanam's religious and social zeal was the religious and philanthropic work of the institution and propagation through the world of the Society of St. Vincent de Paul. That Society, which now numbers 140,000 active members, may fairly be taken to represent the most perfect scheme of lay charity for the help of the poor which has emanated from the Church in modern times. At once religious in its spirit and democratic in its organization and methods, it is the abiding and best memorial of Frederic Ozanam—Catholic and Democrat.

CHAPTER VI

OZANAM AND CHRISTIAN DEMOCRACY

CHAPTER VI

OZANAM lived in an age of revolution. Charles X. had been driven off the throne by the followers of Voltaire and Rousseau, whose sophisms and fallacies had shaken the faith of the greater number of Frenchmen in Divine Providence. Louis Philippe, who succeeded him, called himself " King of the French," not King of France. He was a trimmer, who believed in compromise so as to please both parties in the State. He smiled sweetly at the Clerical and Monarchical parties, and winked confidentially at their opponents. He promised to hold the balance equally between them, and hoped to profit by the mistakes of both sides.

Scepticism was the predominant note of the educated classes, Reason was accepted as the judge of all truths, and Religion was laughed at as the folly of mankind, a superstition only fit to be believed in by women and children. The professors in the Colleges and Universities were all free-thinkers, and scoffed at the idea of Divine Revelation as childishness.

The position of Catholics like Ozanam was a difficult one when he was appointed as a professor in the Sorbonne. The Catholic party had always been allied to those of the Legitimists and the nobility, the landowners of France. These had never studied the interests of the agricultural classes, who paid the taxes which supported the State. The first French Revolution would not have succeeded as it did had it not been for the general dissatisfaction caused by the exactions of the Farmers General of the Taxes appointed by Louis XV. The people generally welcomed the new Government as deliverers from an intolerable yoke of oppression. The new Government called itself " Liberal " and preached a new doctrine of Liberty and Equality, promising all kinds of reforms of abuses, which were much needed. Many of the young generation in the Colleges and most of the middle classes adopted Liberalism as their party, hoping through it for a new heaven and a new earth. Lamennais, Lacordaire, and Montalembert were Liberals, and even a few of the clergy here and there. Ozanam himself, although detesting the irreligious teachings of the leaders, admitted that there was some logical truth in some of their theories —such as the natural equality of men. But this could only exist in an ideal Republic where all were animated by the same spirit of justice and friendship. He had long dreamed of an ideal Republic organized by a Christian Democracy,

Government by the people for the people. But he soon realized by experience that such an ideal was not possible in a world in which men were only moved by selfishness and jealousy. The example of the Apostles in Jerusalem, when the first Christians had all things in common, was no longer practised in the nineteenth century, except in Monasteries and Convents. There all the inmates were equal and all goods were in common, and the Abbot was only *primus inter pares*. The theory was therefore practical under certain circumstances. But he found that the fallacies of Rousseau had taken possession of the popular mind, and until their foolishness and futility had been demonstrated, the ideal could never be realized; and yet something must be done if society and even Christianity was to be saved. Some effort must be made to save the common people from the dangerous doctrines of Socialism which were preached. He wrote to the members of the Conference: " Put yourselves, as Pius IX. is trying to do, at the head of all reasonable movements, and convert the people, as the pagans were converted at the fall of the Roman Empire, by showing the people your faith, your sympathy, and your example. I have always believed, when matters were at their worst, in the possibility of Christian Democracy—indeed, as far as politics go, I believe in nothing else. The true principle," he said, " was the self-sacrifice of each for the benefit of all, and this is the basis of all Christian charity. Let the working classes understand that the Church is the mother of all classes, and perfectly unbiassed in her affection for all men."

The results of the Revolution of 1848 were an appalling state of destitution in Paris, for over a quarter of a million of the workmen were unemployed, and the distress of their families was extreme. Here was a great opportunity for the Brothers, and he urged them to embrace it. They did so nobly, and many rich men collected money for them to help them in their work. " Go and make friends among the poor," he said to them : "give to each family what personal help you can. A better training enables you to assist them ; in one place it will be by legal advice, in another medical. To some you may give practical advice, for others you may procure work. In all cases help them to help themselves, and consider it your primary duty, whether you take them tickets for relief or not, to render them some personal service."

And this has been the practice of the Conferences of St. Vincent de Paul ever since in all parts of the world. It is the only practical form of Christian Democracy which is possible.

Whether Ozanam's forebodings of a great struggle between Labour and Capital is to be fought out in England or America the future alone will show.

The efforts of the Socialists of late years point to

their hope of a great international strike—a war of the
classes. The Socialistic forces, true to their origin,
are diametrically opposed to the Catholic Church.
The new paganism hates both Catholic principles
and practices; instead of brotherly love, it teaches
self - love. It denies Revelation, the supernatural,
and the authority of the Church. It exalts the
Seven Deadly Sins into Civic Virtues. Here the
work of the brothers can be of great aid to the
Church. In their visits to their cases they can see
that the children are baptized and attend Mass and
Catechism on Sundays, and that when they leave
school they get Catholic situations; that they
associate with Catholics in clubs, etc., and that they
regard the brothers always as friends and advisers.

The annual reports sent by the Conferences to
the Councils prove how generally these works are
carried out.

The personal friendship of the brothers with the
poor, their courtesy and helpfulness, will have more
weight than the flimsy sophistries of the Socialists.
The common sense of the working man will show
him that all the advantages offered to him by them
have been already provided by the care of the
Church. He will look upon the Socialists as upon
blind men groping helplessly in the dark after an
ideal which exists before them. As a plain fact, the
community in which are found the ideals of true
Liberty, Equality, and Fraternity is the Catholic

Church itself. I believe, as did Ozanam, that the Society of St. Vincent de Paul is destined to become a great international power in the future, the greater as it is perfectly disinterested, and as free from national or party prejudices as was the " Good Samaritan " in the Scriptures, the prototype of the Society of St. Vincent de Paul.

CHAPTER VII

AIDING CATHOLIC EMIGRANTS

CHAPTER VII

AIDING CATHOLIC EMIGRANTS

In his speech at the Ozanam Centenary at Manchester, Cardinal Bourne urged upon the Society the necessity of assisting Catholic male emigrants in choosing where to settle, and, if possible, to select particular centres, and in places where Catholics were numerous. Emigrants going out in twos or threes were liable to be absorbed into non-Catholic communities. He added: " No greater work of charity could be committed to the Society of St. Vincent de Paul than this of looking after Catholic emigrants."

In this matter the Conferences both in Great Britain and the Dominions can render useful assistance. The Dominions are calling out for emigrants and offering great inducements to settlers. But they do not think much of the religious requirements of Catholics.

To show that the importance of this work has been appreciated by our Colonial Conferences, I give here an extract from a circular which has been

addressed by the Superior Council of Australasia to
the Superior Councils in Great Britain and Ireland:

"SOCIETY OF ST. VINCENT DE PAUL,
"SUPERIOR COUNCIL OF AUSTRALASIA,
" 176, PHILLIP STREET, SYDNEY,
" 21st *February*, 1913.

" SIR AND DEAR BROTHER,

" I am instructed by the Superior Council of
Australasia to ask you tó kindly inform the Presidents of Conferences under your Council that letters
of introduction to us from Presidents of our Society
given to Catholic immigrants to Australia or New
Zealand will receive special attention from us. We
shall do our best to help them in every way, temporally
and spiritually.

" The addressee of the letter of introduction had
better be, of course, the President at the port at
which the immigrant is to land. I can answer for
it that everywhere his reception will be cordial. I
send you a copy of our latest Annual Report, con-
taining the names and addresses of our Presidents,
though a letter simply to the President without any
name would easily be delivered. Any priest, and
almost any Catholic, could direct the bearer.

" We, here, know that there is no very great need
for aid to our co-religionists on landing. They can
obtain employment in a few days as a rule, and
religion is diffused here as in the Old World. Any
sensible Catholic man landing in one of our cities

need be no more at a loss or in danger as to his
religion than he would be on landing in Liverpool.
But it is always much better to have an introduction
to a Catholic friend; and some classes of labour do
not find employment as rapidly as others, and so
a local helper may be useful.

"And in the case of lads, we would do our best
to see that they were placed with Catholics, and to
look after their faith and be their friends afterwards
as long as they wished.

"Yours truly,

"L. F. Heyden."

At one of the sectional meetings of the National
Catholic Congress held at Plymouth, Brother P. E.
Smyth, of Melbourne, stated that in Victoria the Conferences were taking up the work practically. They
were surprised to see so many Catholic emigrants
arriving in the colony, and they were doing their
best to meet their requirements. He said they had
300 Conferences of the Society who were all anxious
to get in touch with Catholics arriving. He suggested
that the names of proposing emigrants, with the
dates of their sailing, and the ports at which
they would arrive, should be communicated to the
Conferences at those ports.

There can be no doubt that the Conferences of
the Society in all other parts of the British Empire
will be equally desirous of receiving and helping

Catholic emigrants. Statistics show that the majority who leave Great Britain go to the provinces of Canada, in consequence of the great advantages offered to settlers. Now, the Catholic Church is very strong in some of the provinces of Canada, and relatively weak in others. The distances between Catholic missions are so great in some districts that it is practically impossible for Catholics to secure the blessings of their faith except at great sacrifices of time and money.

I have no doubt that the numerous Conferences in the United States will gladly co-operate in so practical a work of Catholic charity.

I feel sure that if Ozanam were alive he would encourage to the utmost an apostolic work of this nature. But I think also that he would advise its extension to other parts of the world beyond those of the British Empire and the United States. He would point to the fact that so many thousands of emigrants leave Italy, Spain, and Central Europe every year to settle in the United States, Brazil, etc. Would not the same organization render priceless services to those emigrants also? No doubt that also will come to pass in due course.

The fruitful soil of the Society of St. Vincent is constantly bringing forth abundant crops of good works, suited to the needs of the different countries in which the Conferences are settled. These works are always indigenous to their native soil. But thi work of assisting Catholic emigrants is one of international importance, for we are living in an age of national unrest, similar to that which flooded Europe in the first centuries of the Christian Era and overturned the mighty Roman Empire. The descendants of those barbarian tribes of Goths, Huns, and Vandals are as restless as ever, and they are bent upon peopling the New World. It is fitting, therefore, that the Conferences of St. Vincent de Paul, as the friends and brothers of the poor, should be privileged to render the emigrants fraternal advice and assistance, both when leaving and when arriving.

The Report of the Board of Trade shows that the number of passengers from the United Kingdom to places outside of Europe in 1912 was 656,835. Of these 28·8 per cent. were foreigners, and of these probably about half were Catholics, and no doubt poor, as they travelled in the steerage. Of the British emigrants 74·5 per cent. were about to settle in other parts of the Empire, and 23·4 per cent. went to the United States. The Canadian Agency states that in one week there arrived at Winnipeg 3,868 emigrants, of whom 2,610 were British. It will be noticed therefore how vast a field is opened for Catholic charity by this great emigration movement. The great need is to group Catholic emigrants in such districts as where Catholic families are already settled, and where Catholic churches and schools are to be found. If Catholic fervour is to be maintained

it can only be by the emigrant associating with
Catholic neighbours. There is no surer way of
extinguishing a fire than by scattering the embers
of it. There is no reason why Catholic villages
should not be formed in some of the colonies, a
certain number of families undertaking to settle in
one district and to unite to provide for the main-
tenance of a priest and church. This has been
practically carried out in several of our distant and
smaller colonies with good effect.

In the United States there are many colonies of
Germans, Italians, Spaniards, Poles, Greeks, etc.,
all of which support their own schools, native priests,
and churches, and all with success. It is a great
international movement of historic importance, and
one in which the great International Society of
St. Vincent de Paul should take a leading part.

Ozanam, in one of his letters to Wigley, alluding
to the collapse of one of the communist settlements in
the United States, wrote: "Nevertheless, I believe
that the principles upon which the community was
founded were correct. It failed because it was lack-
ing in the spiritual cement which is composed of the
feelings of self-sacrifice, brotherly love, and justice.
Perhaps we shall see established some day a truly
Catholic settlement upon one of those vast prairies
of the West, under the guidance of one of the great
Orders like the Benedictines or the Chartreux, in
which all benefits shall be equitably shared among

the members under the stewardship of the monks.
That such a system of community of goods existed
among the Apostles and Disciples in Jerusalem in
the first century is proved by the words in the Acts
of the Apostles. Not otherwise can the stern judgment of St. Peter upon Ananias and Sapphira be
explained."

In another letter he wrote :

" The experience of the Franciscans in Mexico,
and of the Jesuits in Paraguay, prove the possibility
of insuring the happiness of the people here and
hereafter where justice is guided by religion. But
when selfishness and cupidity are allowed to rule,
unhappiness and failure must result. . . .

" In your own country, as in Gaul, the monks
were always the instructors in agriculture. We find
that the farmers who cultivated the Abbey lands were
always more successful than they who worked for the
nobles. And so I hope that some day the English
or the Americans, with their well-known practical
spirit of initiative in which we Frenchmen are want-
ing, will find districts in your vast and fertile colonies
upon which will be founded truly Catholic communities and cities under the ægis of the Church, as of
old. This would be the fulfilment of my old dream
of a Christian Democracy. . . .

" The Christian family is the unit, the State is the
multiple; this is a truth which should be impressed
by the Conferences upon the cases whom they visit ;

it will help them to realize the true meaning of the words ' Equality ' and ' Fraternity.' "

Wigley was at the time a member of a small group of young men who sympathized with the new school of the pre-Raphaelites in Art, and followed the dicta of Ruskin, William Morris, and Rossetti, as Gospel utterances. Ozanam denounced the spirit of these as pure paganism, and hoped that the Society of St. Vincent de Paul in England would produce from its colleges, as in France, young writers who would uphold in the Press and in lectures the ancient claims of the Catholic Church as Mother of Arts, Letters, and Civilization.

So many of Ozanam's prophecies and aspirations have been fulfilled that we may hope that some day defenders of Catholic interests may arise from the ranks of the Society of St. Vincent de Paul. But it must be remembered that the Society takes no glory in this world for the works of her children. She gives the inspiration for the good work, the brothers carry it out as best they can.

I think it only just in this place to put upon record some of the works which have been carried on in England by the brothers of the Society outside of those of the Conferences. The first, which was introduced by Brother Wigley, was the Society of St. Francis Regis, whose work it is to obtain from parents, etc., the certificates of consent to the marriages of their children, etc., as required by